# THE PATH TO PUPILLAGE

*A Guide for the Aspiring Barrister*

"Anyone aspiring ... COLLEGE LEARNING RESOURCE CENTRE
invaluable book"
**From the Foreword by The Right Honourable The Lord Ph...**
**of Worth Matravers, President of the Supreme Court of the**
**United Kingdom**

"*The Path to Pupillage* is an invaluable compass for any budding pupil
and its publication could not be timelier"
**Chris Milsom, in *Counsel*, October 2008**

"… a modern networker's pocket book and justifiably heavy on detail,
with a great glossary and splendid sections on funding and resources
which are directly relevant for the modern trainee barrister"
**Philip Taylor, MBE, in *The Specialist Paralegal*, Summer 2008**

# THE PATH TO PUPILLAGE
## *A Guide for the Aspiring Barrister*

Second Edition

By

**Georgina Wolfe and Alexander Robson**

**SWEET & MAXWELL**      THOMSON REUTERS

First edition 2008
Second edition 2010

Published in 2010 by Thomson Reuters (Legal) Limited
(Registered in England & Wales, Company No 1679046.
Registered Office and address for service:
100 Avenue Road, London, NW3 3PF) trading as Sweet & Maxwell

For further information on our products and services, visit
www.sweetandmaxwell.co.uk

Printed by Ashford Colour Press Ltd, Gosport, Hants
Typeset by LBJ Typesetting Ltd of Kingsclere

No natural forests were destroyed to make this product;
only farmed timber was used and re-planted.

**British Library Cataloguing in Publication Data**

A CIP catalogue record for this book
is available from the British Library

ISBN 978-0-414-04236-0

Thomson Reuters and the Thomson Reuters logo are trademarks of
Thomson Reuters. Sweet & Maxwell ® is a registered trademark of
Thomson Reuters (Legal) Limited.

# FOREWORD

I came to the Bar after reading law at Cambridge. I had no contacts in the law and little idea about how I would start to make my way as a barrister. I had joined the Middle Temple because I was told that they gave the best scholarships. In those days you had to eat 36 dinners over three years before you could be called to the Bar. Usually you found yourself dining with other students. There were no activities after dinner. Dining seemed a waste of time. One evening, however, I found myself sitting next to two barristers. They asked me about myself. When they discovered that I had done National Service in the Royal Navy one told me that he practised in Admiralty Chambers and suggested that I should do a pupillage with him. He was called Barry Sheen and in due course he became the Admiralty Judge. I had not even heard of Admiralty Chambers, but I leafed through the law reports and found that Barry Sheen appeared frequently in the Admiralty Court. So I accepted his offer of a pupillage, and that was followed by an offer of a seat in Chambers, which I also accepted.

How different life is today. A series of hurdles has to be crossed by anyone who wants to practise at the Bar, and each seems higher than the one before; and most who seek to cross these are encumbered by an ever-growing mountain of debt. This mountain will now have to be just a little bit higher, for anyone aspiring to practise at the Bar will wish to purchase this invaluable book. It covers every step to pupillage, from the initial decision to aspire to the Bar, the different paths to choose from, the merits of the rival Inns, and the scholarships they offer, the different ways of acquiring the learning in the law that the profession requires, vocational training, the different ways of gaining experience, both as an advocate and outside the law, and finally how to set about gaining that vital pupillage.

Not everyone can or will succeed, but this book will help you to follow in the footsteps of the authors, who write from their own experience in achieving pupillage. Give it your best effort, for I believe that there is still no career that offers more satisfaction. Jonathan Sumption's "view from the top" in Chapter 2 tells you why—and he survived a pupillage with me.

*The Right Honourable The Lord Phillips of Worth Matravers,*
*President of the Supreme Court of the United Kingdom*

# DEDICATION

*Dedicated to*
*G.M.W.*
*and*
*J.N.R. and G.C.R.*

# ACKNOWLEDGEMENTS

The authors would like to thank the many people who have helped in the preparation of this book including:

Adam King, Afua Hirsch, Alex Aldridge, Alex Deane, Alison Gerry, Alistair Richardson, Alix Jackson, Andy Roy, Arianna Pozzuoli, Azeem Suterwalla, the Bar Standards Board, the Bar Council, Barney Branston, Benjamin Moody, Bernard Richmond QC, Brennagh Smith, Bridget Forster, Carolyn Smart, Chris Newman, Christa Richmond, Clare Heaton, Clare Rider, Colin Wynter QC, Corinna Ferguson, Damien Walker, Daniel Thomas, David Herling, David Lascelles, Edward Mallett, Eleanor Searley, Fiona Burrough, Fiona Fulton, Frank Walwyn, the Honourable Mr Justice Vos QC, George Spalton, Giles Cannock, Gill Robson, Gwion Lewis, Guy Holborn, Hui Ling McCarthy, Inga Deakin, James Duffy, James Rivett, James Robson, James Wakefield, Jennifer Sauboorah, Jennie Gillies, Joanna Robinson, John Furber QC, Jonathan Sumption QC, Joseph Sullivan, Judith Kendra, Judith Rogerson, Julian Gregory, Karl Mackie, Kathryn Pickard, Kathryn Perera, Kerry Finch, Kevin Toomey, Krystle Mullin, Leila Benyounes, Lee Reynolds, Lord Grabiner QC, Lord Neuberger of Abbotsbury, Lord Phillips of Worth Matravers, Lucie Briggs, Marion Howard, Martin Palmer, Mary Page, Maya Lester, Michael Mylonas, Michael O'Sullivan, Miles Copeland, Naina Patel, Naomi Wiseman, Neil Robson, Nicola Robson, Nicholas McBride, Nicki McLaren, Niki Iatrou, Oliver Rawlins, Owen Davies QC, Philip Evans, Quinn Clarke, Richard Mott, Richard Sear, Richard Tetlow, Richard Wald, Robert Christie, Robert Forrest, Robert Harland, Robert Purves, Rosie Budden, Ruth Holtham, Dr Ruth Smith, Sally O'Neill QC, Samreen Akhtar, Sara Mansoori, Sarah Corman, Sasha Blackmore, Second Cup Queens Quay West, Shu Shin Luh, Simon Myerson QC, Simon Ramsden, Stephen Migdal, Susan Harrop, Susie Darling, Susannah Jones, Tessa Hetherington, The Black Sheep, Tim Kevan, Tom Alkin, Tom Butler, WeirFoulds, the trustees of the Harold G. Fox Scholarship, Constance Sutherland, Nicola Thurlow, Claire Sharp and Sweet & Maxwell.

Grateful acknowledgement is made to the following authors and publishers for their permission to quote from their works:

'The Job I'd Like Best' taken from *Just William: Home for the Holidays*, by Richmal Crompton. Reprinted by kind permission of A P Watt Ltd on behalf of The Executors of the Estate of Dr Paul Ashbee.

# CONTENTS

# SECTION 1:
# A CAREER AT THE BAR

# barrister (ˈbærɪstə)

A lawyer who has been called to the Bar of England and Wales.

# pupillage (ˈpjuːpɪlɪʤ)

The barristers' apprenticeship.

# 1 WHY THE BAR?

*by Colin Wynter QC, Devereux Chambers*

That is a question that will be asked of every applicant for pupillage and I have received any number of different answers when I have asked it.

When I was asked the same question some twenty odd years ago, I remember being stumped for an answer. Should I give as my reason "Perry Mason", "Rumpole" (both TV lawyers) or should I proclaim a burning desire to right the wrongs of the world? The truth was that I didn't know very much about what barristers did, other than as dramatised on television, but I did know that it was a respected profession of high standards in which hard work, application, determination and (as later became apparent) timely dollops of good fortune, could take a person as far as his or her abilities allowed. That to me, as a young (and black) law student in the early 1980s, was a liberating and inspiring notion.

Entry to the profession now seems, at least anecdotally, to be harder than at any previous time. Numbers seeking to join the profession are up at the same time as the number of available pupillages is down. The statistics may prove daunting to some. If there is a consolation it is that the playing field is much more level now than it has ever been and applicants for pupillage can generally be assured that if they demonstrate the greatest ability and potential during the various chambers' recruitment processes, they will succeed in securing a pupillage, irrespective of their particular background.

There will be times during your career when you will feel out of your depth, when your mind may go blank and when you will lose cases that you (and worse, your solicitor) will think you should have won. You will have to pick yourself up, dust yourself down and head on to the next case. The self-confidence found in most barristers is a necessary trait, since barristers work alone and must find encouragement from within. Even the most quiet and reflective barrister will possess a strong inner confidence in his or her ability.

The Bar is a profession which, in the long term, rewards hard work and perseverance. By working hard and giving always of your best, you will be in a position to take advantage of the various strokes of luck which will happen your way throughout your career.

Good luck!

# 2 THE VIEW FROM THE TOP

*The Right Honourable The Lord Neuberger of Abbotsbury,*
*Master of the Rolls*

A career at the Bar should be both rewarding and enjoyable, at least for those with the right temperament and the requisite talents. What is the right temperament? I suggest a combination of honesty, courage, commitment, high spirits, perseverance and stamina. As to the requisite talents, I would list analytical skills, intellect, quick-wittedness, persuasiveness, organisational skills and fluency—and, as always in life, the ability to grab luck as it comes your way. That is not to say that you cannot succeed unless you have all these qualities, but honesty is essential, and it would be a severe disadvantage if you lacked any two of the others.

Highlights of a career at the Bar are multifarious. Some of the following events may not occur, and the precise order may vary, but, from my experience, the highlights are along these lines. First, there is the offer of a pupillage, the initial rung on the ladder, which justifies your commitment to the BVC. Then there is the first time your pupil master sends out in his or her name a document (such as an Opinion or a Statement of Case) which you prepared. That is a sign that you have begun to grasp the paperwork side of things. Next, there is your first time on your feet in court; your baptism of fire, perhaps the most important moment in terms of drama. Around the same time, there is your first conference—a client coming to you for advice—they are starting to take you seriously. You are then invited to become a member of chambers: a vital event, as near as you get to finding security at the Bar. Then there is the first solicitor to ask for you personally to advise or appear in court; that is the beginning of your practice. Next, a judge recognises you from a previous case, so you are beginning to become a habitué of the courts. Some time there will be the first case which you should lose, but which you win: you now really are an advocate. Stretching beyond that is your first five-day case (a test of commitment and organisation), your first appearance in the Court of Appeal (a test of nerve), your first reported case (fame at last, at least among the distressingly few people who notice), increasing numbers of demanding and interesting cases (hard work, but you pick up technique as you go along), and, who knows, high profile, ground-breaking cases followed by QC status and appointment as a judge.

Of course, it isn't highlights all the way, however lucky and able you are. There will be the run of losses, the wrong advice, the occasional shortage of work, the boring cases, the apparently rude and stupid judges, the unreasonable clients, the difficult colleagues, the demanding clerk, the feeling of being overwhelmed. All these features are inevitable from time to time, and this explains why high spirits are so important.

*Sally O'Neill QC, former Chairman of the Criminal Bar Association*

The Bar was not my first choice of profession and I came to it as a rather reluctant student, intending really just to do pupillage and then take stock. As I suspect many of the readers of this book have found, however, practice at the Bar can be wonderful, particularly, in my case, at the Criminal Bar and I soon found myself hooked. I had no contacts at the Bar when I was called, my best and most useful contact was Gray's Inn which was a great support to me in the early days, both in pupillage and in finding a tenancy, and I owe it a great debt of gratitude.

The particular highs for me have all been about what happens in court. The pleasure when a cross-examination works, the sheer entertainment of watching someone else's cross-examination go spectacularly and sometimes hilariously wrong, the gratification of feeling that the jury has listened to your closing speech and the relief when the jury return a verdict which is in favour of your client. I still remember with pleasure many years ago being complimented by the judge and my opponent on my cross-examination of a defendant. I had really prepared it carefully in the sort of way Bar students and pupils are now taught to but we weren't. On that occasion it worked but the key is definitely preparation. Another highlight was when a very junior member of the Bar defending complained to the judge after my re-examination of a witness that I had just undone all his hard work in cross-examination! It rarely works like that as you will no doubt find out and I won't describe the other occasions when I have been unwise enough to re-examine and it hasn't worked.

One of the major benefits of the Bar is being able to trust your colleagues and rely on their integrity. Don't let it get personal. There is nothing worse than doing a trial with an opponent that you don't get on with. Integrity and courtesy are two of the qualities I value most at the Bar but it is also great fun. We are lucky indeed to be able to be in a profession which enables us to try to achieve a just result for our clients whilst still doing a job which we love. Long may it last.

*Jonathan Sumption QC*

What attracted me to the Bar, after some years of teaching history, was the absence of a prescribed pecking order. You rise (or fall) as fast as your personality and skills allow. Experience of course is a plus, but mere seniority is not.

With this goes total responsibility for your own work. No one looks over your shoulder, to check that you are doing it right. After pupillage, you don't submit your thoughts to someone further up the line, to be reviewed and sent off under his own name. For good or ill, it is your opinion or your submission, and your reputation which turns on its quality. That is exhilarating, and rarer than you might think.

Of course, these are features of the profession that carry risk. But luck is a necessary element in any successful career, not just at the Bar. What can fairly be said is that it is much rarer for real talent to be overlooked at today's Bar than it was a generation ago.

Two pieces of advice. First, don't get the idea that legal practice is all about law. Law is just common sense with knobs on. Most legal disputes are really about facts. They are a great deal more interesting, and once those have been correctly analysed, the legal answer is usually obvious. Second, don't imagine that the Criminal Bar is the only place where you will encounter real life. Clients and their problems are just as fascinating and a great deal more varied in other fields. Some of the other fields pay better too.

*Lord Grabiner QC*

Being a barrister is the best job in the world. You have the chance to work independently on wonderful cases and have an interesting and fulfilling career. I have loved it.

Every generation throws up people who want to do their own thing and yearn to be advocates. Only a few get really far at the Bar and thousands will not make it. To be successful, you need a desire to be an advocate and to be your own boss. You need independence, resilience and drive, and a willingness to work very hard. You've really got to want to do it. It is not a matter of feeling you might quite fancy it—it must be in your bones.

I recommend going to a Magistrates' Court. It will teach you some tricks of advocacy and give you a flavour of how people behave: who's lying, who's telling the truth, who's frightened, who's evasive. Sit there for a day to see first-hand what goes on and decide if it's for you. Remember, however clever you are, you can still be a rotten advocate.

As a student in the 1960s, the image of the Bar scared me. Back then it was a class-ridden profession and, truth be told, I was a bit nervous of it all. I had not been to public school or Oxbridge. I was at the LSE and the short walk across the Aldwych seemed quite a big stride between what I perceived as two very different worlds. I need not have worried. Chambers look for academic excellence and the potential to be a good barrister. Solicitors are interested in making sure that their clients get someone who knows what they are doing. Everything else is irrelevant.

Barristers come from very diverse backgrounds. What matters is what you are capable of and how well you do your job. Don't ever let perceptions and stereotypes deter you from coming to the Bar.

*The Honourable Mr Justice Vos QC, Former Chairman of the Bar Council*

I believe that success at the Bar demands five main qualities in addition to high ethical standards and tenacity: a good academic mind; incisiveness providing a swift route to the heart of a problem; an ability to deal with people; presentational skills; and organisational discipline.

The job satisfaction for those who succeed is second to none. In crime and family work, you are able to make a real difference to the lives of some of the least privileged members of our society. In my practice, I have handled some of the most fascinating and high profile disputes. I specialise in chancery and commercial work, which produces a spectrum of disputes allowing the advocate an insight into other worlds. I have been able to spend periods of time learning about matters ranging from genetic engineering to the written Chinese language and Francis Bacon's entire oeuvre. Most jobs neither enable nor require you to understand so many different kinds of business and human endeavour. I can only describe what barristers do as truly a privilege. It is worth the effort and dedication that is required to succeed.

# SECTION 2: FIRST STEPS TO THE BAR

# 3 A DOSE OF REALITY

*By Bernard Richmond QC, Lamb Building*

The decision to become a barrister is not one to be taken lightly. As well as the financial pressures involved in the early years, there is no guarantee that you will even be able to get a foot on the first rung of the ladder—pupillage.

It is deemed "anti-competitive" to do anything to limit the number of people qualifying as barristers (through the various institutions providing the BPTC). This means that, every year, there are some 3,500 people fighting for approximately 500 pupillage places.

If you get a pupillage the statistics improve—approximately 400 tenancies a year and the remainder of those who get through pupillage find good jobs in a legal context.

Before you start, however, you need to think long and hard about the skills needed to make sure that you are in the "500" and not the remaining 3,000. Tough as it is, this means that you'll have to take a realistic look at your skills and weaknesses; then compare them to the skills required to be a barrister.

Some professions are an elite—not because they should be limited to people from certain social classes but because they demand a degree of intellectual ability and associated skills. Being a barrister is one such profession. If you don't like public speaking or you are not good at expressing yourself orally then practice in a branch of the profession requiring excellence in advocacy is not for you.

If you are not adept with the English language (both orally and in writing) then there is no realistic prospect of success in a profession where words and language are our main tools.

The practice of law involves a large amount of problem solving and analysis within a legal context. If you are not a strong lawyer or you lack analytical skills then, again, the modern Bar is not a place where you will succeed.

Those who are successful combine aptitude with drive and determination. If you aren't interested in developing your skills in every way possible, in undertaking mini-pupillages to gain valuable insight and experience and, essentially, in demonstrating that you want to be a barrister more than anything else, then you are unlikely to impress chambers when they come to decide whether to select you for interview and pupillage.

Finally, it's expensive. There are scholarships and loans which make things a bit easier and pupillages are funded; however, it is a costly business and debts can mount up if you are not vigilant. Being realistic about your finances is, therefore, as important as being realistic about your skills.

On the other hand, if you have the ability, talent, drive and determination then do not let anyone deter you. It is the most amazing and inspiring job and I can think of nothing else I'd rather be doing!

*An Unsuccessful Pupillage Applicant:*

I had gone through life hitting all the academic targets—straight As at school, a place at a top university and a good degree. I was surprised by the calibre of students I met on my GDL course but I was always confident that I would get a pupillage. I worked hard, I did extra-curricular activities, minis and mooting and despite all the doom and gloom I'd heard about how hard it was to get pupillage, I wasn't in any doubt that I would be snapped up. I was frankly shocked when the rejection letters started arriving. Of the 40 applications I had sent off, I got four interviews and ultimately no pupillage. The feedback was pretty unanimous—they said I was good but others were better.

People will tell you how hard it is. To be honest, I didn't listen; I simply didn't think that it applied to me. Everyone told me that I would make a great barrister and I believed them. I spent tens of thousands of pounds chasing this dream. I will try again but now I really don't know if I will ever make it and I have had to give some serious thought to what I can do next. I wish someone had told me how hard it really is—not just told me the statistics but looked at my CV and pointed out that I might not be up to it—but if they had, I wonder if I would have listened.

| Academic Year | 00/01 | 01/02 | 02/03 | 03/04 | 04/05 | 05/06 | 06/07 | 07/08 |
|---|---|---|---|---|---|---|---|---|
| BVC Graduates | 1082 | 1188 | 1121 | 1251 | 1392 | 1480 | 1560 | 1720 |
| Pupillages commenced | 695 | 700 | 698 | 518 | 556 | 515 | 527 | 562 |

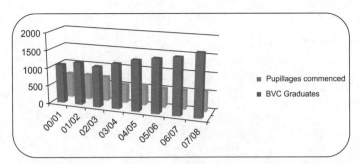

Source: adapted from *www.barcouncil.org.uk/trainingandeducation/CareersHome/ TheStatistics*

---

**Number of pupillage applicants who do not get a single interview: 51 per cent**

Source: The BVC (Bar Vocational Course) Student Survey on Aspirations for Practice at the Bar conducted by the Bar Council

# 4 WHICH WAY TO THE BAR?

**The Overview**

| Year | Law Degree | Non-law Degree |
|------|-----------|----------------|
| 1–3 | Degree course | Degree course |
| 4 | Bar Professional Training Course | Graduate Diploma in Law |
| 5 | Pupillage | Bar Professional Training Course |
| 6 | Third-six/Tenancy | Pupillage |
| 7 | Tenancy | Third-Six/Tenancy |

**The Future Barrister's Timetable**

Many legal publications offer timetables to assist you with applications but these tend to be limited to the strict essentials of application deadlines. This timetable includes more extra-curricular activities which you can do to give yourself and your CV the earliest advantages. If you are a mature student, read the university-related sections for ideas which you could investigate in the year before you begin law school.

All terms and acronyms are defined in the Glossary at Chapter 28.

*During University*

- Get as much law-related experience as you can: volunteer to take part in mock trials in the law department; visit the local law courts; attend careers fairs and talk to solicitors; and talk to any barrister that crosses your path (see Section 4).

- If you are not reading law, the point above is especially important. If possible, take a law elective and speak to law students about their studies.

- Take advantage of the long university holidays to get some legal work experience, anything from helping out in your local solicitors' firm to trying out a vacation placement (the solicitor's equivalent of a mini-pupillage). It does not have to be connected to the Bar (although if you find something Bar-related, all the better) (see Section 4).

- Get people-centric experience particularly in fields where you are helping people tackle their problems: volunteer for your university Night Line (a nationwide listening service run by students for other students); and volunteer to help out with homeless charities, Amnesty or any charities with a legal element (see Chapter 14).

- Try some amateur acting. Most universities have some student drama and it provides a great opportunity to overcome the inevitable stage fright and practise public speaking.

- Take up debating for your university. There are debating competitions almost every weekend of the year and two major annual international competitions (the European and the World Championships) to which your university might send a team (see Chapter 13).

*For Non-Law Graduates: Final Year of University or the Year Before You Begin the GDL*

- Get the prospectuses for the law schools which interest you; attend their open days.

- Apply for your GDL (the deadlines tend to be in February).

- Start applying for mini-pupillages in the fields of law that you think you might be keen to practise (apply for as many as you can). Undertake any which you are offered (see Chapter 11).

- Spend some time giving serious thought to your chosen career and whether you are 100 per cent set on going to the Bar.

- Attend careers fairs.

- Join an Inn and apply for GDL scholarships (see Chapter 5).

*GDL Year or Final Year of a Law Degree*

- Get the prospectuses for the BPTC law schools and attend their open days.

- Apply for your BPTC (the deadlines tend to be early in the calendar year) (see Chapter 10).

- Apply for BPTC scholarships through your Inn and law school.

- Continue to apply for mini-pupillages in the fields of law that you think you might be keen to practise (apply for as many as you can). Undertake as many as you can fit in around your legal studies (see Chapter 11).

- If you have not yet joined an Inn, join one (remember it is compulsory to join one before May of the year you are to begin the BPTC).

- Make a list of all the chambers that you are interested to apply to and note down their application deadlines in your diary to ensure that you do not miss any (some are very early in the year). Double-check all the dates by looking at chambers' websites as those published on the Pupillage Portal may not be up-to-date.

- Seek all the legal experience you can.

- Attend any chambers' evenings or open days available.

- Attend the Target National Pupillage Fair, which usually takes place in March at the beginning of the application season.

- Start mooting and, if you did not try it at university, debating (see Chapters 12 and 13).

- Begin your qualifying sessions and use them as opportunities to speak to barristers and other students (see Chapter 5).

- Enter essay competitions (see Chapter 15).

- Volunteer for pro bono work for example through the Citizens Advice Bureaux, Legal Advice Centres or FRU (see Chapter 14).

- Consider any other legal work that you can do and, if you have time, do it (see Chapter 15).

- Apply for pupillages for the first time, both through the Pupillage Portal and to chambers outside the system (see Chapter 21).

- Revise for pupillage interviews (see Chapter 22).

- Do a mock interview (See Chapter 22).

- Take advantage of the summer where you may be tied to England or Wales by interviews and get more legal work experience such as paralegaling in a City firm (see Chapter 15).

- If you can get away, consider spending time in an overseas jurisdiction, for example working with Death Row prisoners (Reprieve and Amicus offer such opportunities; see Chapter 15).

- If you are not successful in securing pupillage, apply for the Pupillage Portal Clearing Pool.

*The BPTC Year*

(Unless you have pupillage, and, remember, most candidates will not:)

- Continue mini-pupillaging, FRU, debating, mooting, CAB work, entering essay competitions and doing any other legal work you can find.

- Again attend the Target National Pupillage Fair.

- Talk to some friends who were successful at getting pupillages the first time round and ask for their advice.

- Apply for overseas scholarships (see Chapter 5).

- Prepare to reapply for the next round of pupillage applications.

# 5 THE INNS OF COURT AND SCHOLARSHIPS

If you wish to become a barrister, you must become a member of one of the Inns of Court (Inns). There are four Inns: Lincoln's Inn; Inner Temple; Middle Temple and Gray's Inn.

> To those who do not know them, the Inns of Court can seem a very strange, outmoded and exclusive institution. If you have never experienced them, it is hard to imagine what possible relevance they could have. As you become more familiar with what we do, and we welcome all students willing to work towards success at the Bar, the Inns become one of your professional points of reference. In some ways, you might compare their function to that of a medieval guild: a professional body whose members share professional expertise and ethos, passed on from the experienced members to those still learning.
>
> *Christa Richmond,*
> *Deputy Under Treasurer (Education), Middle Temple*

The term "inn" originally referred to a town house or mansion which was used as a hostel for students, providing education, housing, food, a library and a chapel. The earliest known reference to the individual Inns of Court is in a manuscript of 1388, which mentions the appointment of members of the Inner Temple, Middle Temple and Gray's Inn as Serjeants-at-Law. Nowadays, the Inns offer students such benefits as advocacy training, financial assistance in the form of scholarships (see below) and hardship funds, and subsidised food and entertainment in Hall. Lincoln's Inn and the Middle Temple also provide subsidised housing for a few students who have been awarded scholarships.

There are three categories of Inn member:

- "Masters of the Bench" or "Benchers": elected for life, these are High Court judges, circuit judges or senior QCs, as well as a few distinguished juniors. They constitute the governing body of the

Inn. Some people of particular eminence are elected as honorary benchers who play no active part in the governance of the Inn.

- "Hall": this group includes all members of the Inn who have been called to the Bar. Those who play an active part are likely to be barristers or judges, but those who have gone on to work in other professions are not excluded.

- Students.

An Inn's members share professional expertise and ethos, all under-pinned by lively collegiate activity. In practical terms, this means support for students from the moment they join.

On admission, students are offered the option to be allocated a sponsor, a practitioner who is not intended to act as a tutor or welfare officer, but is always ready to be consulted when spondees need advice, even if only to suggest who is the right person to approach for further help. Getting a sponsor and keeping in contact with him or her is a very good idea.

*Christa Richmond*

### Qualifying Sessions

In order to be called to the Bar of England and Wales, you must attend 12 "qualifying sessions" organised by your Inn. Traditionally, these were a fixed number of dinners (originally 48 and reduced over the years to 12) eaten in your Inn, at which you socialised with other members. Today, your qualifying sessions can still include dinners but you may also attend other educational sessions including lectures or an advocacy weekend at Cumberland Lodge, a country house in Windsor Great Park. This weekend is highly recommended by all who go.

The qualifying sessions which students need to attend provide a good example of the way in which the Inns combine collegiate and educational activities. They may be linked to lectures by senior members of the Inn or distinguished guests, or to moots, or to advocacy training which is provided by experienced practitioners, but they may also consist of a dinner and concert, or even dinner and dance—all geared towards making you feel a part of a profession which is both learned and friendly. All qual-ifying sessions have that purpose, though some events are specifically designed to encourage the students and the senior members of the Inn to mingle.

In addition to the 12 qualifying sessions which students are obliged to attend (and many attend over 12 as they really are very good value in more ways than one), students are invited to take part in mooting and debating competitions, to practise their advocacy in sessions in which barristers are trained to be advocacy trainers, to act as witnesses in advocacy workshops for young barristers who already have some court experience. These are good opportunities not only to learn about the law and about advocacy, but to make contact with practitioners and fellow students which may turn into lasting professional and personal friendship. The Bar is a demanding profession: having the friendship and support of your colleagues at all levels of seniority is an essential part of remaining sane!

*Christa Richmond*

*A Pupil*
The 12 qualifying sessions were really good fun—far from the chore I feared that they would be. I went to dinners, the mooting final, excellent lectures and, one of the highlights, a music night with Humphrey Lyttleton. My favourite qualifying session was the advocacy weekend at Cumberland Lodge, in the beautiful grounds of Windsor Castle. We spent the weekend improving our advocacy with some of the best practitioners and teachers in the Inn and indeed at the Bar, making new friends and admiring the impressive Lodge and its art collection. We even met the Queen!

As soon as you join your Inn, you can begin your qualifying sessions. It is important to make a good impression on all the barristers you meet during these sessions. You may come across a member of a future inter-view panel. This can be catastrophic if they remember that you inappropriately staggered into them after too many drinks, but a huge help if you made a good impression.

*A Pupil*
Studying in Nottingham, I was concerned about how to complete all the 12 qualifying sessions in London. However, I very quickly realised that I could be in close contact with my Inn without studying just round the corner and I was surprised how easy it was to do the 12 sessions. The Inn

organised advocacy programmes, dinners and guest lectures to take place
in Nottingham which could count as two qualifying sessions. When we
did go to London it was for a day of lectures, lunch and dinner—
squeezing lots of qualifying sessions into one trip.

*Choosing your Inn*

Choosing your Inn is a decision that you should make as early as possible
and no later than May of the year you begin your BPTC.

> **Note:** Your Inn does not have any effect on the choice of chambers to which
> you may apply for pupillage. It is entirely possible and extremely common
> to be a member of one Inn but to practise in chambers located in a different
> Inn or out of London.

All four Inns provide essentially the same services and educational
programmes. All offer a library and a restaurant/bar. Some organise
annual mooting and debating competitions for students. The Inns inspire
a certain patriotism in their members and it is extremely rare to hear a bad
word against any of them. Most barristers agree that ultimately it does not
matter which Inn you join—all are excellent.

To help you decide on an Inn, here are some of the facts and figures
about each of the Inns of Court.

## Lincoln's Inn

> *"London. Michaelmas Term lately over, and the
> Lord Chancellor sitting in Lincoln's Inn Hall."*

> The opening lines of *Bleak House* by Charles Dickens

The Inn was probably named after Henry de Lacy, third Earl of Lincoln,
whose arms gave the Lincoln's Inn badge its lion.

Famously, Lincoln's Inn is one of only two places where the Loyal
Toast (the first toast after a formal meal where diners stand and raise their
glasses to the toast "The Queen") may be taken sitting down (the other
being the Royal Navy). Legend has it that this privilege was granted in
perpetuity because, one night in 1672 when Charles II was dining in the

Inn, it was impossible to find a Bencher sober enough to stand for the toast.

## Lincoln's Inn Facts and Figures

*Number of student members each year*: approximately 700.

*Scholarship fund*: Total of approximately £1,342,000 (not means-tested). 300–350 apply annually for BPTC scholarships; approximately 110–120 BPTC scholarships are awarded. 70 students apply annually for GDL scholarships; approximately 35 GDL scholarships are awarded.

*Famous members*: Tony Blair, Benjamin Disraeli, William Gladstone and Margaret Thatcher are among the 16 former Prime Ministers whom Lincoln's Inn counts amongst its members. Other famous past members have included Lord Denning, Wilkie Collins, John Donne, Mohammad Ali Jinnah and Thomas More. Nelson Mandela is an honorary Bencher.

*Notable features*: The Inn welcomes students aspiring to all fields of practice, and past members include many distinguished common lawyers. The opening chapter of *Bleak House* highlights the Inn's strong connections with the Chancery Bar. The Court of Chancery frequently sat in the Old Hall until the Royal Courts of Justice were opened in 1882, and to this day most of the leading Chancery chambers are in the Inn.

The Inn also has strong European connections, reflected in its student programme. The current British judge on the European Court of Human Rights is from Lincoln's Inn, as have been all his predecessors since 1980, and there has been strong representation from the Inn at the European Court of Justice. Student visits to Strasbourg and Luxembourg are a feature, extended recently to the international courts at The Hague. "Euro-evenings" are regularly held, with the annual Thomas More lecture being a highlight.

## Inner Temple

*"A gentil Mauniple . . . of a temple"*

Geoffrey Chaucer in *The Canterbury Tales*

Inner and Middle Temple surround the Temple Church. This round Church, which shot to fame in Dan Brown's *The Da Vinci Code*, was built by the Knights Templar. After the Knights were abolished by Pope Clement in 1312, lawyers moved into the Temple, and the Middle and Inner Temples were formed. The Knights, though long gone, are not forgotten and the figures of two Knights, both riding a single horse, can be seen as a bronze statue in the western end of Church Court, outside Temple Church. It may be that the image evolved into Inner Temple's emblem: the winged horse or Pegasus. However, it is more likely that Pegasus was adopted in honour of Lord Robert Dudley, favourite of Queen Elizabeth I and her Master of the Horse, who participated in the 1561 Inner Temple Christmas revels.

Much of Inner Temple was destroyed in the Great Fire of London in 1666, with further damage occurring in subsequent fires and the Blitz. Although the Hall, Treasury Office, Benchers' Rooms and Library have all been reconstructed since World War II, King's Bench Walk running along the eastern side of the Inn remains a fine example of seventeenth-century architecture.

### Inner Temple Facts and Figures

*Number of student members each year*: approximately 450.

*Scholarship fund*: Total of approximately £1,230,000 (85 per cent of scholarships are means-tested according to family income—the remaining 15 per cent are fixed scholarships of pre-defined amounts; all applicants are interviewed). 250–300 apply annually for BPTC scholarships; approximately 80–100 BPTC scholarships are awarded. 60–70 apply annually for GDL scholarships; approximately 30 GDL scholarships are awarded. There is a guaranteed funding scheme whereby students who have successfully obtained a GDL award, who complete the GDL and go on to take the BPTC will, on application, automatically receive an award of the same amount for their BPTC year without further interview.

Holders of GDL awards are also welcome to apply for a higher award for the BPTC year which will not jeopardise their right to the guaranteed amount.

*Famous members*: Clement Attlee, James Boswell, Geoffrey Chaucer (reportedly), Sir Francis Drake, Mohandas Gandhi (disbarred in 1922 and reinstated in 1988), Sir John Mortimer and Bram Stoker. Inner has also produced the last five Lord Chancellors. Royal members have included George VI, James II and the Duke of Edinburgh.

*Notable features*: Inner Temple has played host to a number of films and television productions including the BBC's Vanity Fair and David Copperfield.

Inner Temple has a strong history of student mooters and debaters with past students among the champions at both European and World Championships. Inner also holds annual "Inter-Varsity" competitions in both mooting and debating in which members of the other Inns and universities may compete.

One of Inner Temple's student schemes is the Police Liaison Scheme which is an excellent opportunity for those interested in criminal or police law to shadow a police officer for a day. Its societies range from drama, mooting and debating to football.

## Middle Temple

*"Within the Temple Hall we were too loud;
The garden here is more convenient"*

Shakespeare's *Henry VI*, Act 2, Scene 4

Although Middle Temple's own records date back to 1501, the Inn was probably in existence several centuries earlier. In the Lincoln's Inn Black Books of 1442, there is a record of payment for a wine party with the Middle Temple.

Middle Temple Hall was completed in 1573 and boasts a stunning double hammer beam roof carved from oak from Windsor Forest. The intricate wooden screen dating back to 1574 was painstakingly restored following damage during World War II. In 1602 the Hall played host to the first performance of William Shakespeare's *Twelfth Night* and the fountain outside was immortalised in Charles Dickens' *Martin Chuzzlewit*.

The Middle Temple "Cup Board", upon which new barristers sign their names in the Call Book, supposedly comes from the forehatch of Sir Francis Drake's ship The Golden Hind, the lantern of which hung in the entrance to Hall until it was destroyed in an air raid in 1941.

The Middle Temple badge is a lamb on a red cross—another legacy from the days of the Knights Templar.

## Middle Temple Facts and Figures

*Number of student members each year*: approximately 600–650.

*Scholarship fund*: Total of approximately £1,000,000 (all applicants who secure a place on the relevant course are interviewed, size of award depending on individual financial situation, plus student accommodation in Clapham). Approximately 360 apply annually for BPTC scholarships; approximately 150 BPTC scholarships are awarded (and about 45 entrance exhibitions). About 60 apply annually for GDL scholarships; approximately 35 GDL scholarships and 10 entrace exhibitions are awarded.

*Famous members*: Edmund Burke, Charles Dickens, Henry Fielding, Sir Martin Frobisher, Sir Walter Raleigh and William Makepeace Thackeray. Queen Margrethe II of Denmark became an Honorary Bencher in 1992. Royal Benchers of the past include King Edward VII, King Edward VIII, Queen Elizabeth, the Queen Mother and Diana, Princess of Wales. Prince William became a Royal Bencher in 2009.

*Notable Features*: After he parked his trailer in the Middle Temple garden during the filming of *The Da Vinci Code*, Tom Hanks replaced the Inn's lawn. You might recognise some of the corridors surrounding the Hall from the Bridget Jones films.

Middle Temple holds the annual Rosamund Smith Mooting Competition, judged throughout by Middle Temple Benchers with the semi-final and final rounds held in Hall after dinner before a panel of senior judges. The finalists each receive a wig and gown and a mooting trip to the USA.

Middle also holds an annual debating competition for student members with the final held in the Hall after dinner. Middle Templars are among the past victors of the World Debating Championships.

Each year before Christmas, the Middle Temple hosts the Revels, a medley of songs and comedy skits performed by students, Hall and Benchers.

## Gray's Inn

*"to Gray's Inn where I saw many beauties"*

The Diaries of Samuel Pepys

Gray's Inn is the smallest of the Inns in terms of membership. It has traditionally been seen as the most progressive of the Inns, being the first to introduce student advocacy training and other such initiatives. It evolved from the first habitation known to have been around the site of the present Hall: the Manor House of Sir Reginald de Grey, Chief Justice of Chester, Constable and Sheriff of Nottingham. This is also probably where the Inn got its name and the alternative spelling ("Gray" rather than "Grey") is believed to have come about when Dr Johnson's dictionary standardised spellings in 1755. The Inn originally used the de Grey arms which can still be seen in the pediment above the Benchers' entrance to the House premises. Today the badge is a sable griffin segreant or a golden griffin on a black field.

The records of Gray's Inn start in 1569 but evidence of its existence dates back to 1388. Gray's has suffered more war and fire damage than any of the other Inns; indeed, between 1680 and 1687 it survived no less than three fires. One such fire destroyed the library. When it was rebuilt, it was said to be "the most comfortable library in London" but unfortunately it was razed again in 1940. Master Winston Churchill opened the current library in 1946 and described it as "the architecture of the aftermath".

The war damage to the Hall was minimised by the temporary removal of many items such as the windows, Treasurers' shields and even the sixteenth-century walls, all of which were reinstated and remain today. According to tradition, the screen at the west end of the Hall came from wood from a Spanish galleon given as a gift by Queen Elizabeth I.

Gray's Inn has seen its fair share of writers and playwrights. Shakespeare was a regular in Hall (his patron Lord Southampton was a member of the Inn) and the young Charles Dickens first started work in Raymond Buildings to the west of the Inn.

Gray's Inn Gardens, known as "the Walks", were laid out by Sir Francis Bacon in 1606 when he was Treasurer of the Inn.

Gray's Inn Facts and Figures

*Number of student members each year*: 350.

*Scholarship fund*: Total of approximately £795,000 (merit based in the first instance, means may be considered thereafter). 120 apply annually for BPTC scholarships; approximately 55 BPTC scholarships are awarded (highest awards £17,000; lowest awards £5,000). 20 apply annually for GDL scholarships; approximately 17 GDL scholarships are awarded.

*Motto*: *Integra Lex Aequi Custos Rectique Magistra Non Habet Affectus Sed Causas Gubernat* (Impartial justice, guardian of equity, mistress of the law, without fear or favour rule men's causes aright).

Famous members: Sir Francis Bacon, Sir Winston Churchill, Thomas Cromwell and Lord Howard of Effingham (the Admiral who famously defeated the Spanish Armada in 1588). Queen Elizabeth I was the Inn's Patron Lady.

Notable Features: Among other things, Gray's Inn offers a choir, a croquet club, a golfing society and a football club.

**Dining**: You may have heard rumours of some of the more idiosyncratic dining traditions of the Inns. These have been greatly relaxed in recent years but there are one or two for which it is worth being prepared.

A friend of my brothers is going to be a lawyer. You learn to be a lawyer by eating dinners in a temple. This sounds to me a very nice way of learning to be anything and I think I should make a very good lawyer. I'm certainly very good at eating dinners and it must be great fun to eat 'em in a temple. Then when you've eaten enough dinners you go about sending people to prison. Which must be great fun. It's sort of like a policeman but higher because a lawyer has an office to do it in but the policeman does it in the street.

*Just William Home for the Holidays* by Richmal Crompton

- Students dining in the Inns wear black gowns similar to those worn by barristers in court. These are provided by each Inn before you enter the Hall.

- Diners sit in groups of four, called "messes". Traditionally, the top right-hand member of the mess had the role of "Captain" and served the others their food.

- In Middle Temple you are not permitted (in theory at least) to speak to anyone outside your mess. Meals are now served by the Inn staff and no longer by the mess Captain.

- In Inner and Middle, no one may enter or leave the Hall until the second grace.

- Gray's Inn was, until recently, famous for its "challenges". These are no longer compulsory but remain open to volunteers. Challenges involve standing on the table and singing a song, reciting poetry or telling a joke.

- In Gray's Inn, while the barristers may drink wine, port or sherry, students may only drink water and wine.

*A Pupil*
I was surprised to find that dining was a lot of fun—so much fun that I started bringing guests. The food was delicious, particularly at one lecture where we were offered little pots of fish and chips! All the events were excellent value; I am sure there is nowhere else in London that you could get a three course meal with wine and entertainment for so little, particularly in such a grand setting.

Further information about the Inns is available on their respective websites and from their educational officers (see Chapter 29 on Resources).

**Inns' Scholarships**

The Inns give over £4 million worth of scholarships and prizes to aspiring barristers in England and Wales each year. Being awarded a scholarship not only provides students with essential financial support through the expensive qualifying years but also gives their CVs a huge boost.

*A Pupil*
Having worked hard at university, I achieved a good grade. I enjoyed mooting and was determined to become a barrister but my parents

weren't able to help pay for my education. The expense of the BVC seemed prohibitive and I was worried I would have to delay my legal studies in order to afford it.

I applied for a scholarship not knowing what to expect. When I arrived at the Inn I was already nervous and felt further daunted by its grandeur but the interviewers really put me at ease. Some of the questions were very challenging and I had no idea how I'd performed.

A few weeks later the Inn wrote to inform me that I'd been successful. My scholarship award went a long way towards covering my fees. It was still a very expensive year, but the cost was more manageable. The prestige of the scholarship felt like a green light from within the profession which gave me a lot of confidence.

**An Important Note:** While you can apply to an Inn for a scholarship prior to joining as a student member (which you must then do should you be awarded a scholarship), you are not permitted to apply for scholarships to more than one Inn each year. Should you attempt it, any scholarships awarded by any of the Inns will be revoked.

If you were unsuccessful in applying one year, you are not precluded from applying to another Inn the following year provided that you are not a member of the original Inn.

The scholarship process for all the Inns is by means of an application form followed by a round of interviews. The application forms can be downloaded from the Inns' websites.

The only Inn to interview all candidates is the Middle Temple; the three others interview only those who make the grade on paper. Note that if you do not have a place on the BPTC, you may not be interviewed for a BPTC scholarship.

**Means-Testing**: Middle Temple is the only Inn to operate a complete means-testing policy for their scholarships (Inner's scholarships are also 85 per cent means-tested to allow for seven named scholarships of fixed amounts). This policy is designed to ensure that scholarship funds go to those most in need. However, it does not disadvantage a financially secure student: a student can be awarded the most prestigious scholarship with only a token amount of money as the figures for scholarships are not fixed. The amounts awarded to each scholar are not published.

*GDL Scholarships*

For those who did not take law as an undergraduate degree, there are scholarships available to assist with your GDL year. With only a handful of successful candidates, GDL scholars have something to give their CV an edge right from the beginning.

Many would-be candidates are preoccupied with other things (final exams, full-time work or summer holidays) during the application and interview process so your chances of success can be higher than you might think.

The GDL Scholarship Interview

Interviews can vary greatly, even within the same Inn. The panels tend to be made up of about three senior practitioners, often Masters of the Bench. More than anything else, the panel is keen to see that you are interested in the law and committed to a career at the Bar. They are looking for candidates with intelligence and a spark who will be an asset to the Inn.

If you find yourself in the position of being offered a scholarship interview, give some serious thought to the reasons why you want to be a barrister—the question is almost guaranteed to come up in some form. The panel does not expect you to know everything about any area of law or to commit yourself to a field of practice, but it may help if you are able to explain why an area appeals to you.

*BPTC Scholarships*

Based on volume of applications, scholarships for the BPTC are more competitive than those for the GDL. That said, there are considerably more scholarships, and more money, on offer.

The BPTC Scholarship Interview

As an applicant for a BPTC scholarship, you will have had some legal training and you should expect to be cross-examined on this. The panel might select a field that interests them or one which has recently made the headlines. Make sure that you are clued up on recent legal developments and that you have a view on anything controversial which has recently been in the legal or national press. They might also ask if a particular practice area interests you. As with GDL scholarship interviews, you are not expected to know an entire field of law inside-out, nor to commit yourself to one, but you should be able to explain where your interests currently lie and why. Remember not to say anything that you cannot substantiate.

Points to prepare before scholarship interviews:

- Think about an area of law that interests you and why it appeals.

- Read the newspapers every day in the run up to the interview, paying particular attention to the legal pages. Think about the issues raised so that you have a view on them.

- Re-read your application form and try to anticipate any potential areas on which you might be questioned.

- Scholarships interviews tend to be very similar to pupillage interviews; read the advice in Chapter 22.

## Overseas Scholarships

The Inns offer a selection of overseas scholarships including visits to India, America and Canada. These vary in length from three weeks in India (The Lady Templeman Indo-British Goodwill Award of the Middle Temple) to ten months in Canada (the Harold G. Fox Scholarship, open to students from all Inns). Overseas scholarships involve an application process with interview much like the scholarships described above. They offer the unique opportunity to work within a different legal system and can be generously remunerated. Note: for some overseas scholarships, you must have been called to the Bar.

# SECTION 3: TRAINING

# 6 LAW DEGREE V LAW CONVERSION COURSE

Before you can begin pupillage, you must complete two stages of training: the academic stage and the vocational stage (the Bar Professional Training Course, "BPTC", formerly know as the BVC).

For the academic stage there are two main options. Either you can study law as an undergraduate degree or do a non-law degree followed by the Graduate Diploma in Law (the "GDL").

Whichever path you take will not affect your chances of getting pupillage and approximately equal numbers of students take each route. Both options are now equally respected by the Bar and pupillage committees do not appear to demonstrate a preference. A quick glance at any number of junior tenants' CVs on chambers' websites will reveal almost identical numbers took the law degree as took the GDL.

However, there are several factors which you might wish to consider when you make your decision.

| Pros of a Law Degree: | Pros of a Non-Law Degree Followed by the GDL: |
| --- | --- |
| • You will gain a deeper understanding of the law because you will spend at least three years immersed in it, thus providing a longer period to grasp the subject.<br><br>• Gives you longer to decide which area of law you would like to practise.<br><br>• You have the opportunity to study niche areas such as tax or international law which are not usually | • Allows you to choose and study a degree subject for enjoyment and academic interest if your first choice is not law.<br><br>• Gives you a more rounded education and demonstrates an interest outside the law.<br><br>• Gives you more time to accumulate legal and non-legal work experience.<br><br>• The law may be fresher in your mind when you start pupillage; you will have studied all areas more recently than law graduates |

available on the GDL. This gives you a greater idea of which area you might ultimately wish to practise.

- This is a faster route to becoming a barrister.
- You will get an excellent qualification which can also open the door to a non-legal career.
- You will spend three years in the legal world (albeit the academic legal world), enabling you to meet people and make contacts.
- This is the least expensive route to the Bar.

who may not have looked at some subjects since their first year.

- You will probably make an extra group of friends on the GDL which may be particularly valuable if you have moved to a new city for the first time with a view to practising there.
- Having chosen the longer route, you probably come to law with more life experience than an undergraduate fresh from a law degree—an attribute that is valued by pupillage committees.

Cons of a Law Degree:

- Does not give you the additional breadth of knowledge or the added skills you may learn from another degree.
- As few students will have taken law at school, committing to a law degree is a risk—there is a chance you may not like the subject.
- Unless you are a mature student, you may come to the Bar relatively young and with less life experience than the slightly older candidates. It may be harder to demonstrate maturity and experience on your pupillage applications.

Cons of the Non-Law Degree Followed by the GDL:

- Expense—a degree plus the cost of an extra year's fees (the GDL can cost up to £7,000 in fees).
- You have a very short time (a matter of months) to decide which area of law you are interested in practising before the application process begins and you will not have time to investigate any aspects of particular interest.
- There is a large amount of law to take in and memorise in a short time. With pupillage applications thrown in on top, this can be a very tough year.

There is also a third, lesser known postgraduate option: the "senior status law degree". Currently offered by just over twenty universities, this two-year graduate course is promoted under various names such as LLB Senior Status or BA (Hons) Senior Status. In some respects this course appears to offer the best of both worlds: a longer period in which to study the law without taking the full law undergraduate degree. Bear in mind that this route is not especially favoured by chambers. It is also the longest way to qualify.

*A former BVC Student*

I took the GDL part-time and it was such a good idea that I did the same with the BVC. I was working and wanted to spend more time with my family so part-time study was an excellent option for me. It has also meant that I have had longer to undertake legal work experience and mini-pupillages so I now feel ready to give pupillage applications my best shot.

Studying part-time has taken much longer but, unlike other professions, there is no stigma attached to coming to the Bar as a mature student or after a first career—if anything, it is actually seen as an advantage. Being able to work while on the courses has also meant that I can avoid falling into debt while I qualify.

# 7 THE SEVEN FOUNDATIONS OF LEGAL KNOWLEDGE

Seven areas of law are deemed so important that you must have studied them in order to qualify as a barrister or solicitor in England and Wales. These areas constitute the bedrock of your legal education whether you choose to study a law degree or the GDL. They are called the "seven foundations of legal knowledge" but are more commonly referred to as the "core subjects". The following definitions and examples are intended to be for guidance only and are therefore simplified.

| Subject | What is it? | Practical Examples of a Typical Legal Issue |
|---------|-------------|---------------------------------------------|
| Constitutional and Administrative | The law governing the relationship between Parliament, the Executive and the Judiciary; the legal mechanisms for controlling the actions of public bodies (principally "Judicial Review"). | Parliament passes a law saying that all blue-eyed babies must be killed at birth. Cleopatra's baby, Antony, is born with blue eyes. Cleopatra objects to Antony being killed. What can the courts do to help? |
| Contract | The law governing agreements made between two or more people or companies. | Bonnie promises to fix Clyde's car if he pays her £100. Clyde pays her the money. Bonnie decides not to fix the car but doesn't tell Clyde. The next day Clyde goes to his driveway to find his car still broken. As a result, he misses an important final round job |

| Subject | What is it? | Practical Examples of a Typical Legal Issue |
|---------|------------|---------------------------------------------|
| Contract—*cont.* | The law governing agreements made between two or more people or companies—*cont.* | interview and so misses out on the job. Can Clyde be compensated for losing the chance of getting the job? |
| Criminal | The law restricting the commission of harmful acts such as murder, theft or rape. | Judy insults Punch. Punch, who is very drunk, pushes Judy hard to get her away from him. Judy falls backwards into the road, is run over and dies. Has Punch committed murder? |
| Equity and Trusts | The law that applies where one person owns something but is required to use it for the benefit of another. | Juliet leaves all her money to her lover Romeo in her will, specifying that Romeo must use it for the education of Juliet's daughter. Romeo decides to keep the money and spend none of it on Juliet's daughter, whom he doesn't like. What can the courts do? |
| EU | The law about the government of the European Union and the relationships between EU countries. | EU Member state Neverland decides it has too many residents from its neighbouring EU Member state Lilliput and that it is losing its national identity. It therefore blocks its borders to all Lilliputian citizens. Gulliver is from Lilliput and wants to join his wife living in Neverland. What can he do? |

| Subject | What is it? | Practical Examples of a Typical Legal Issue |
|---|---|---|
| Land | The law governing the ownership and use of land and buildings. | Porgy and Bess fall in love. Porgy buys a house, planning for the two of them to live there happily ever after. Porgy works long hours in a big bank. Bess does lots of DIY, builds a garage, generally cares for the property and cooks Porgy dinner each night. After six years Porgy and Bess fall out and decide to separate. The house is sold for double the price Porgy paid for it. Should Bess be entitled to any of the money from the sale of the house? |
| Tort | The law about civil wrongs, such as negligence, the commission of which normally results in money ("compensation") being paid to the person who was wronged. | Jekyll, a young professional footballer, goes for a routine operation at the hospital. The surgeon carrying out the operation, Hyde, did not get any sleep the night before because his neighbour was having a very loud party, and refused requests to turn down the music. Because he is tired, Hyde botches the operation, leaving Jekyll paralysed. Can Jekyll sue Hyde for the money he may have earned as a footballer? Can Hyde sue his neighbour for keeping him awake? |

Whether you choose to study a law degree or a GDL, you will study all of these core subjects. On a degree course, you will also study a range of other subjects such as family law, employment law or international law. You may also have the option of studying one of these core subjects to a more advanced level.

# 8 THE LAW DEGREE

## The Law Degree: An Overview

A qualifying law degree is designed to teach you:

(i) what the law says in certain areas;

(ii) how to apply this established law to new factual scenarios;

(iii) how to research law; and

(iv) how to analyse the existing law in order to see how it could be improved.

You will study the seven core subjects (see Chapter 7), as well as seven other areas of the law that interest you.

A qualifying law degree is valid for starting the BPTC for a period of seven years after you graduate. In theory, therefore, you can apply for the BPTC at any stage within that time. You should be aware, however, that a long delay in practising law after qualification may mean that the knowledge and skills that you developed during the degree have faded with time.

## Applying to Read Law

There is a great range in the quality of tuition, facilities and students between different universities in England and Wales. BPTC providers and barristers know this and so should you. This should be a major factor when selecting where you will study so take a look at a university league table to see which universities are currently ranked most highly. Consider aiming for the best university that your exam results will allow.

Precise entrance requirements for the law degree vary between universities. At almost every university, however, the law degree is one of the most competitive undergraduate courses. Full details are provided by the Universities and Colleges Admission Services (*http://ucas.com*), which is also where you apply for your degree. For admission to a part-time undergraduate law degree course or a senior status law degree for graduates, applications should be made directly to the university or college of higher education offering the course.

## *GCSE, A-Level or International Baccalaureate (IB) Choices*

Younger students are often concerned about which subjects to choose for GCSEs, A-Levels or the IB. The best advice is that, so long as the subjects you choose are academic in nature, you should select those subjects that you enjoy and in which you think you will get the best grades. There is more leeway where GCSE and IB choices are concerned as you take more subjects and therefore there may be room for a non-academic choice. Ensure, however, that the main focus of your studies is academic.

If you have any concerns or questions about which subjects to choose, speak to your teachers or careers advisers, and check the universities' websites. If you cannot find the information you are looking for on a university's website, you could email a specific question to its admissions office.

## *The National Assessment Test for Law (LNAT)*

For some of the top universities in the country, applicants must now sit the LNAT (the acronym mirrors the American equivalent, the "LSAT"). This online test is run by a consortium of UK Universities. It is designed to aid admissions tutors in their assessment of applicants by testing applicants' powers of reasoning and analysis. Testing begins in September of the academic year in which you make your UCAS application. You can choose a date to take the LNAT at a test centre near your home, school or college. Be aware that different universities have different deadlines for completion of the test. Check their websites for more information.

### Tips for the LNAT

1. Practise
It is essential that you practise as much as possible before sitting the LNAT. Use the website (*www.lnat.ac.uk*) to download past tests. There are books that have been written specifically to help students succeed in the LNAT (see Chapter 29 on Resources). Make use of them.

## 2. Prepare

One part of the LNAT is an essay from a list of topics. This essay is not marked centrally but is sent to the admissions officers of each university to which you are applying. You can assist yourself greatly by reading widely before sitting the test. Read the newspapers every day, including the editorials. Try to get a range of perspectives: perhaps contrast a Left-leaning paper (such as the Guardian) with a more Conservative approach (such as the Daily Telegraph). This will help you in two ways. First, it should bolster the substance of your answer by improving your general knowledge. Secondly, you will see how a tight, punchy argument is constructed.

## 3. Watch the clock

The LNAT is timed so plan in advance how long you can spend on each question. It is crucial that you resist the temptation to exceed your time on one question thinking you will be able to make it up later. If you are stuck on something, move on to the next question then come back to it if you have time at the end.

## On the Course

Your opportunity to be in the strongest possible position for pupillage applications begins in earnest with your studies on the law degree. Not only is a good result essential to impress pupillage committees, a law degree—if approached in the right way—can be excellent training for life as a barrister. As a barrister, a large part of your role will be to analyse factual scenarios, research the relevant law and then create persuasive legal arguments. You learn all of these skills on the degree course. Whichever university you go to, you should approach your studies with enthusiasm and a determination to get the best grade you possibly can.

### Read the Cases

Barristers rely on an ability to use prior decisions of the courts to support their arguments. This is known as the system of "precedent" whereby, in simple terms, a court is bound by previous decisions of higher courts. Using other cases to substantiate your arguments is a skill you should work hard to develop in your studies.

Some students on a law degree will rely on the analysis of others by reading short summaries of a few cases (or perhaps the headnotes) and one textbook. Doubtless, this is easier and faster than thinking for yourself. However, it is not a good way to prepare to be a barrister. Spend time reading the cases in full. If Counsel's arguments are reported, read them. Make careful notes of the reasoning in the judgments, then, crucially, spend some time thinking about that reasoning. Ask yourself if you agree with the judges' analysis and conclusions, including those in dissenting judgments. You should then read a further discussion of the case in a textbook or case note. These steps are vital if you want to develop the analytical skills that are fundamental to a successful career at the Bar.

You will encounter literally thousands of cases and it is impossible to adopt this more thorough approach for all of them in the limited time you have during your degree. However, be sure to do it for every important case and as many additional cases as time allows.

In judgments of cases there can be lots of explanations about why the law says what it does as well as hints as to what it should say. These are immensely useful and quite impressive to mention in exams. Read the cases themselves—case notes should be a supplement to this and not a substitution.

*Nicholas McBride, Director of Studies in Law at Pembroke College, Cambridge, and author of* Letters to a Law Student

*Discuss the Law*

As a barrister, you will spend much of your professional life talking about the law. Sometimes you will argue complex legal principles before a judge. At other times you will have to explain those same complex principles in clear, non-legal terms to a confused client. In both situations you must be able both to think and to express yourself with clarity.

The law degree is an excellent place to learn these skills, both on the course and through mooting. Try to talk to other people on your course about the law. Bounce ideas around and ask questions about things you do not understand. Many universities have websites where you can discuss law online. If there is not one where you study, why not set one up?

Don't be afraid to get a reputation as someone who takes law seriously and is really hard working: you'll get your reward later on.

*Nicholas McBride*

*Lectures and Tutorials*

Law degrees tend to put a lot of focus on self-teaching. The vast majority of your time will be spent reading independently. It is important that you take advantage of all opportunities to interact with academics and other students. At the very least, this means going to lectures and tutorials. It also means that you should not sit quietly trying not to be noticed. The Bar is not a place for people who are afraid to express their views. It may be a short time before you are in front of an interview panel who could be asking much more difficult questions and where your answer will matter much more. It will help you enormously to talk with fellow students and experts about why the law says what it does and how it could be improved.

**How to Deal with Nerves in Small Group Sessions**
It can be difficult for people who are shy to speak up in small group sessions. I have a lot of students myself who say very little in small group sessions. This isn't because they're not intelligent; it's just because they aren't used to saying things in front of a group and feel embarrassed about making their point known.

My advice to students like this is: just take the plunge. You can never get rid of anxiety unless you do the thing you're anxious about. For the first few times it may be embarrassing and you'll think you made a fool of yourself. But after that these worries go away. You've got to get yourself out there, state your point of view and realise that actually the world isn't going to come crashing down around you. You get confidence from that. If you are naturally shy then just do it—do it for the sake of doing it and you'll find in time that your anxiety naturally disappears.

*Nicholas McBride*

*Exams*

Work really hard during your law studies to get the very best academic results you can: that is what will give you a foot through chambers' door.
*Lucie Briggs, Atkin Chambers*

Whichever university you go to, remember that your final grade is crucial.

Performing well in exams is the most important way of demonstrating your intellectual ability to chambers. It doesn't matter if you could shine in interviews if poor results preclude you from being invited to any. Exams should be at the forefront of your mind from the day you start.

**Tips on Exams from Nicholas McBride**

1. Think about your exams from day one. Get hold of some past exam papers from your law library and read through them. This can be a great time-saver in helping you focus your studies.

2. Try and get to know people in the years above you who've done well in the exams. Tap into their knowledge about how to do well—especially about what the examiners look for.

3. Before your exams, think about the recent developments in each area of law. These developments often form the inspiration for exam questions so knowing about them will help enormously.

4. Include time in your revision for mock exams. These will help you assess your progress and manage your time.

5. When you are in the exam, ask yourself what issues the examiner is trying to raise in the question.

6. If you are doing an essay, make sure your essay actually answers the question being asked. Engage with the question, do not write around it. Try to write something fresh.

7. If you've put the effort in and you've prepared well for the exams then your efforts will usually be rewarded. Try not to get too scared.

# 9 THE GRADUATE DIPLOMA IN LAW: CONVERTING TO LAW

The Graduate Diploma in Law (GDL) gives non-law graduates a brief introduction to the English Legal System and teaches them the seven core areas of law (see Chapter 7). The course can be taken full-time or part-time at over 35 institutions throughout England and Wales.

> **GDL/CPE/Law Conversion:** The GDL is also known as the "Common Professional Examination" (CPE) and the "law conversion course". The CPE is a precursor to the GDL, and, to all intents and purposes, is the same qualification. The terms GDL and CPE are used almost interchangeably by students and practitioners. GDL is used throughout this book. The more colloquial title "law conversion course" refers to the fact that the GDL "converts" non-law students into law students.

The course takes one year full-time or two years part-time. There are up to three chances to pass each exam—although if you are serious about the Bar you should aim to pass first time. After three fails of any one paper you must begin the entire course again or take a law degree. Pass grades are divided into "Distinction", "Commendation" and "Pass".

Like a law degree, the GDL is valid for seven years. This means that if you wish to take the BPTC, you must do so within seven years of graduation from the GDL. If you fail to do so, you can reactivate the qualification either by showing reliable independent evidence of your current competence or by taking a written exam in the seven core areas. See the "Academic Stage" section of the Bar Standards Board website for further details.

All applications for the GDL must be made centrally through the website *www.lawcabs.ac.uk.* The application form is available each November and should be completed and sent off by the February of the calendar year in which you wish to begin studying.

Before you decide that you want to take the GDL, one final thing to bear in mind is that you are cramming the majority of a law degree into 10 months (unless you take it part-time). It is going to be tough.

> Even having spent five years studying for an undergraduate degree and a Masters degree and then working for the UN, the GDL was a very intense year and really hard work.
>
> *Azeem Suterwalla, Doughty Street Chambers*

**Factors to Consider When Choosing Your Law School**

Unsurprisingly, there are pros and cons to each of the law schools and you must select the one which feels right for you. If possible, attend an open day to see the facilities and get a feel for the atmosphere. If a visit is impossible, have a look at their websites and ask for a prospectus.

*Location and Cost*

Consider whether you wish to be in London where you will be close to the Inns of Court and much of the legal world but where course fees and the cost of living are more expensive. Studying out of London can have definite advantages (see Chapter 10).

*Number of Students*

The numbers of students taking the GDL varies considerably between providers, ranging from as few as 20 at Anglia Ruskin University or the University of Keele, to 1,300 at the College of Law (spread out over different locations). The number of students on the course can greatly affect the overall atmosphere; think about whether you would prefer to study at a smaller provider or somewhere larger.

*Reputation*

Although where you study the GDL is by no means as important to pupillage committees as where you took your undergraduate degree, you should still give the decision careful consideration. Is the course known for being tough and therefore well-respected?

*A Former GDL Student (London)*
My GDL year was, academically speaking, the hardest of my life. My fellow students were the brightest people I had ever met and in some cases this was quite intimidating but it did give the course a real buzz. There was a healthily competitive edge which encouraged us to push ourselves and which will undoubtedly help in practice. My law school was an excellent place to train as a barrister, not only because of its long-standing reputation but also because the staff and fellow students offer so much information and support for those aiming at the Bar.

It is also worth finding out, where possible, how many students went on to get pupillage (such statistics should be available from each provider). Ask whether the course is aimed primarily at future barristers or future solicitors. This may affect the sort of activities organised by the law school, for example, whether there are more talks from solicitors' law firms aimed at future solicitors, or chambers' evenings for future barristers.

*Organisation and Course Materials*

Each course will be structured and organised differently. What is the balance between large group lectures and small group tutorials? Is the course taught primarily through lectures, tutorials or both? How is the course structured? Do you need to prepare for a test in the English Legal System at the beginning of the first term or is that taught as part of the course?

Do the providers you are looking at provide course materials? Do these include lecture manuals, casebooks and statute books as well as textbooks? Will you need to make lecture notes or are these provided?

*A Former GDL Student (Birmingham)*
The major advantage of the course for me was that it was extremely 'spoon fed'. The staff went out of their way to make the work as easy as possible for us to keep track of, including outline lecture notes and detailed small group session plans amounting to a personalised work book for each unit taught. I even refer to these notes now I'm in practice.

*Examinations*

How is the course assessed? Does coursework count or is the course 100 per cent exam-based? And how are the exams timetabled—are they back-to-back or spread over a longer period of time?

*A Former GDL Student (Leeds)*
The week-long break in the exams was brilliant. It gave us a much-needed break to recharge our exhausted batteries and do a little more last-minute revision.

*Upgrade to LLB*

There is an increasing trend for GDL providers to upgrade the GDL qualification to an LLB following the completion of the BPTC at the same provider. While this additional qualification will make little difference to pupillage committees (who will understand the upgrade process), it could be an advantage if you wish to practise overseas where the GDL may not be recognised.

*Pro Bono Opportunities*

With several of the law schools offering impressive, sometimes award-winning, pro bono activities, this is an easy way of improving your CV during the GDL year. These can include student-run Legal Advice Clinics, Street Law (where students can work in the community visiting institutions such as schools and prisons to talk on relevant areas of law) and the Free Representation Unit ("FRU"). Investigate pro bono activities and whether a pro bono component is compulsory.

*A Former GDL Student (Birmingham)*
A major bonus was the pro bono programme. The numerous opportunities really boosted my CV. I was offered more than one pupillage at the end of my GDL year and I am sure I had my pro bono work to thank for this.

*Extra Courses*

With competition heating up between the GDL providers, many are now offering students the chance to take a specialist subject. These can include such courses as Evidence and Forensics, Law in the City or Preparing for Practice.

## How to Survive the GDL

You have to get serious—as soon as you start on the GDL. Get your CV into shape. You can distinguish yourself from a large number of candidates by getting the right minis down, going and doing mooting, whatever it may be. You cannot expect people to somehow see through a thin CV and say 'this person has a lot of potential'.

*Tom Alkin, 11 South Square*

The full-time GDL is an extremely challenging year. It is easy to feel overwhelmed by the sheer volume of reading you are required to do—never mind the analysis required to use the information once you have digested it. And that is before you start mini-pupillages and improving your CV. If you feel the pressure getting to you, remember that everybody finds this year difficult, but it is only a year, and in a few months' time it will be over.

> **First Day Tip:** Take a large bag or wheelie suitcase—your course textbooks are heavy and numerous and the plastic bags provided will make for a difficult journey home.

### Academic Advice

Before the course begins, invest in a range of study guides (there are several on the market) and read them. Although you will probably be told that you do not need to prepare anything for the course (beyond perhaps the English Legal System preparation at some providers), this will give you an excellent overview of each area of the law. With an idea of the framework operating within each area, and an understanding of where the course is going, all the lectures and tutorials will become far easier to comprehend right from the beginning.

The GDL is not like university where lectures may be optional. Attend all lectures and tutorials and keep up with the reading. Some courses are structured in such a way that if you fall behind early on you will really struggle later in the year. For example, the law of negligence in tort law involves first establishing that a duty of care is owed before going on to prove the other elements of negligence. If you miss an early class on the duty of care, it will be very difficult to grasp the later concepts. Make sure you catch up anything that you unavoidably miss.

You will find the GDL much easier if you spend regular working hours preparing for tutorials, making notes and keeping on top of the reading throughout the year. You will quickly realise that you do not have time to read every judgment of every case you encounter (you will encounter thousands). Read only the key ones in full and read what your textbooks say about the rest. You will find some books have useful case extracts which helpfully provide the most pertinent paragraphs of a decision.

> **Tip:** Early in the course, investigate the format of exam papers. You will probably not be expected to answer questions on all sections of each area of law. Work out early on how many you will need to answer and then you can start to choose which areas of each subject particularly interest you and invest a little more time in them in preparation for the exams. Always remember to prepare for more questions than you will have to answer.

If you find that you are not fast enough to make sufficiently detailed notes in lectures, arrange to swap notes with a fellow student to fill in any gaps.

*A Former GDL Student (London)*
Within the first few weeks of starting the GDL, I realised that I was not getting enough down in lectures. I write quite slowly and the sheer volume of information being given to us meant that I could not keep up. I invested in a touch typing CD, borrowed a laptop from my law school and taught myself to type during the evenings. Using the laptop in lectures meant I was able to get much more down and having all my notes on computer made it much easier to compile my revision notes come exam time.

> **Tip:** If you are thinking of buying a laptop, enquire at your law school for the best deal. Many law schools and universities offer students discounted computers through their computer services.

See Chapter 8 for further ideas and tips about getting the most from your legal studies. Remember, however, that you do not have the same luxury of time as a degree student—make sure you prioritise.

*Revision and Exams*

Set aside the Easter holidays for revision. With seven large areas of law to cover, there will be plenty to do.

Often you will be given eight to ten questions on an exam paper and from these you may be required to answer just four. Ensure that you have revised more than just four topics as they will sometimes appear combined with other topics or in a different form from the way you had anticipated. By preparing to answer some extra topics you can ensure that you will be able to answer the minimum number of questions. Remember: you may answer three questions to an excellent standard but if you cannot answer the fourth you risk failing.

The GDL is primarily assessed by way of essay questions. You may know the law inside out but if you cannot structure an essay answer you will not do well. As part of your revision, draw up essay plans from past papers (which should be available in your library, online or by request) and, if they are available, compare them with sample answers.

If you have the opportunity and time to take mock exams, do so.

*General Advice*

Make the most of every opportunity offered. When you are struggling to meet essay deadlines and get all the reading done for your next tutorial it is easy to get swamped and miss out on the other things on offer. Try to plan your work each week so that you have time for any chambers' evenings, mooting and debating competitions and other opportunities that are available, as well as taking some time for yourself. With all the work on the GDL it is easy to let these secondary activities give way to your academic work. Don't make this mistake. The competition for pupillage is fierce and the more experiences you can put down on your application forms, the better chance you will have of getting a first interview. Squeeze in mini-pupillages and work experience during reading weeks and in the holidays.

> **Tip:** During the GDL, start dining at your Inn. This will not only give you a head start completing your 12 qualifying sessions, but will also give you the chance to meet barristers and BPTC students who might be able to give you some helpful advice.

Finally, the GDL is a notoriously tough year. Students have always struggled with it and probably always will. It is important to stay positive. Focus, work hard on your studies and aim for a strong performance in exams. But do not let the course get you depressed: pursue non-legal activities, see friends and take time for yourself. Maintaining a balance is key.

# 10 THE BAR PROFESSIONAL TRAINING COURSE

## What is the Bar Professional Training Course?

With effect from October 2010, the Bar Professional Training Course ("BPTC") is the new name for the vocational stage of a barrister's training. The course is likely to remain better known to practitioners by its previous name: the Bar Vocational Course or "BVC". The new name is the most obvious example of the many changes that were made to the course following a major review in 2007–2008. This review, chaired by Derek Wood QC, involved extensive consultation on the perceived short-comings of the previous course. Key modifications include the introduction of a mandatory aptitude test for entry on the course, a reduction in the length of the course from 32 to 30 weeks, the increase in pass mark from 50 per cent to 60 per cent and a rule that only one resit will be allowed. Consult the BSB website for the full report of the BVC Working Group.

The aim of the BPTC remains the same as that of the BVC. In simple terms, the BPTC is a practical course which teaches the academic lawyer how to think and act like a barrister. According to the BSB:

> The purpose of the Bar Professional Training Course is to enable students, building on their prior learning, to acquire and develop the skills, knowledge and values to become effective members of the Bar of England and Wales. As part of the continuum of training, from the academic stage through to pupillage and continuing professional development of practising barristers, it acts as the bridge between the academic study of law and the practice of law. It aims to move the student from the classroom to the courtroom.

*Outline of the BPTC Curriculum*

| Subject | What does it entail? |
| --- | --- |
| Advocacy | Learning how to present your case and argue points of law or fact in a court or tribunal. |
| Conference Skills | Interviewing clients to find out both their problem and desired solution. Distilling often-complex questions of law into a form that is readily understandable. Explaining what are the realistic prospects of the case and managing the client's expectations. Advising on the best course of action taking into account the client's priorities. |
| Drafting | Writing documents such as Statements of Claim, Defences and Skeleton Arguments to give your case the best chance of success. |
| Legal Research | Learning how to identify and research the relevant point of law in a set of facts using a law library and online legal resources. |
| Negotiation | Identifying your client's needs, investigating the other party's position and negotiating in order to reach a mutually acceptable solution outside court. |
| Opinion Writing | Writing a formal, carefully-reasoned piece of legal advice in response to a specific question of law and/or fact. |
| Civil Litigation Evidence and Remedies | The rules of procedure for the civil courts: which parties may bring a claim, when, how and alleging what? Which remedies can the court provide? |
| Criminal Litigation Evidence and Sentencing | The rules of procedure for the criminal courts and the process of sentencing those found guilty. |

| Professional Ethics | Behaving like a barrister: the duties you owe to the court, to your clients and to your colleagues. |
| Resolution of Disputes out of Court | Advising and representing your clients in the various methods of dispute resolution which fall outside the usual judicial process before courts, for example mediation and negotiation. |
| Options Subjects | Different providers offer different options such as family, intellectual property, commercial or employment. This is something to check when deciding where to do the BPTC. |

At every provider, students are taught partly in large group lectures and partly in small group tutorials. Exactly how the lessons are divided, and how many students are in each class, varies between providers. Check their websites for more information.

## Is the BPTC for You?

Think very carefully before choosing to do the BPTC. In terms of both time and money, the cost of the course can be huge. You may need bank loans, scholarships and possibly years of work just to be able to fund it. Moreover, while some unsuccessful pupillage applicants find the BPTC useful in their alternative careers, many do not. Ask yourself: (i) am I totally committed to a career at the Bar; and (ii) do I realistically have the skills and CV that will give me a fighting chance of pupillage? Ignoring these questions can prove to be a very expensive mistake.

*Reflections on Bar School*
Try to be realistic about the costs and benefits of doing the BPTC. It makes most sense if you see yourself at the Bar for the rest of your career. If not, it is a useful stepping stone but think about where you are trying to go and whether there may be less expensive, draining and difficult ways of getting there.

*Afua Hirsch, Guardian Legal Affairs Correspondent*

I sometimes regret doing the BVC. It costs so much money and I don't think I learnt any transferable skills to be honest; I should have done something different. I'd always wanted to be a journalist and this gave me something to write about—but it was an expensive way to do it.

*Alex Aldridge, journalist, Legal Week*

I think the general skills of presenting information with clarity and authority, and being able to synthesise lots of information into something manageable are useful in any profession.

*Fiona Burrough, Save the Children*

The BVC instils confidence in oneself and teaches a person how to conduct himself in a pressured and fluid environment. Many of the skills learnt during the year are easily transferable: thinking on ones feet; adapting to changing circumstances and confident public speaking to name but a few.

That said, I believe that having 'Barrister-at-Law' on your CV is a double edged sword: on the one hand it shows that you are clearly intelligent, but if you are pursuing other options and are at an interview it invites the very obvious question: Why aren't you a barrister? And no matter how you dress it up it is hard to disguise the fact that you did not quite make the grade. This is because there is no other reason to do the BVC, its sole purpose is to train would-be barristers as barristers.

Just before my BVC started there was a pre-course familiarisation visit during which the head of the school told 100+ people, including myself, that only 25% of us would attain pupillage. While we all believed him, no one believed that it would be them. Such is the nature and self-belief of the people that the BVC attracts.

Take a hard look at yourself. Are you good enough to be a barrister? Self realisation is never an easy thing, but it could just save you a lot of time and effort.

*A former BVC student*

## Minimum Criteria

To apply for the BPTC you must have:

(i) at least a 2:2 degree in law, or a 2:2 degree in a different subject and a Pass in the CPE or GDL;

(ii)  achieved or be equivalent to at least band 7.5 in written and spoken English on the International English Language Testing System (IELTS); and

(iii) joined an Inn by May 31 of the same calendar year that you hope to start the BPTC.

These minimum criteria are subject to the discretion of the Director of the BSB, which can be exercised only in exceptional circumstances. Remember, while these are the requirements for entry to the BPTC, many chambers will not even interview those candidates without a 2:1 degree and/or a commendation on the GDL.

In addition to these, there will be a new requirement that all entrants to the BPTC pass a written test, called the Bar Aptitude Test. The test will focus on comprehension, fluency in the English language and critical reasoning. The aim is to raise admission standards.

Your application to the BPTC may be your first taste of the Bar's competitiveness. If you want to be successful in your application you must do much more than simply meet these criteria. Unsurprisingly, BPTC providers are looking for future successful barristers. Be prepared to demonstrate advocacy (both oral and written), intellect, a commitment to a career at the Bar, drive, interpersonal skills and independence.

Applications for the BPTC are made online through one central website, *www.barprofessionaltraining.org.uk*. You may not apply direct to individual providers. Look at Chapter 21 for further advice on applications and be sure to check the website of each of your preferred providers to see their assessment criteria.

> **Tip**: You may put yourself at an advantage if you submit your application in advance of the January deadline. Although providers will not make offers before that date, under the old system many started looking at the forms as soon as they were received. The same may prove to be true under the new system: getting your application in early may give you a better chance of making a good impression.

## Overseas Students

Many students from overseas jurisdictions come to England and Wales to do their BPTC. The same minimum requirements apply. Some providers have different fees for overseas students, so it is important to check with the providers to which you are applying. Overseas students will have to meet governmental entry regulations and have relevant study permits. Consult *www.ukvisas.gov.uk* for more information.

Completion of the BPTC alone does not mean that an overseas student may practise as a barrister in England and Wales. The BPTC confers the title of "barrister" but without higher rights of audience which are granted after the first six months of pupillage. You should check with the jurisdiction in which you want to practise that the BPTC is recognised.

### How to Choose your Provider

There are currently eight BPTC providers in England and Wales. Courses are offered in the following locations: Birmingham, Bristol, Cardiff, Leeds, London, Manchester, Newcastle and Nottingham. From 2010 there will be a ninth provider.

From the point of view of pupillage committees, it does not matter where you do the course: unlike a law degree, most see the BPTC as a qualification which you either have or don't have—not something that is "worth more" from certain providers. However, do not make the mistake of thinking that this means the courses are of equal quality.

Research the providers using their websites. Ask questions at law fairs. Visit providers on their open days. Look at an online discussion forum such as *www.thestudentroom.co.uk*. If you have specific questions, telephone the course administrator (details below).

There are a range of factors to consider when deciding where to apply.

*Cost*

Wherever you choose to take the BPTC, it will be expensive. Tuition fees alone will be a minimum of about £8,500 and you will pay significantly more if you choose to do the course in London. Barristers on pupillage committees understand how expensive the process of training can be: even if you want to practise in London, it is perfectly acceptable to do the BPTC in another city.

> **Note**: BPTC providers' websites may state the previous year's fees. The forthcoming year's fees may only become apparent after you have signed up. Be prepared for this—particularly if you are on a tight budget.

*The Number of Students on the Course*

The number of people on the course will greatly affect its atmosphere. Some providers have over 500 people studying the BPTC each year, while others have as few as 50.

*A Pupil*
There were just over a hundred of us on my course, which, for me, was an ideal number. It meant there were enough people to have a real variety of backgrounds and interests, but also that everyone could get to know each other. The atmosphere was very friendly and it made us feel as if we were one big team, which made the gruelling pupillage application season a lot less lonely!

*A Pupil*
With about 650 students on my course, you could be sure that there was a group of people with whom you would get on. Also, with so many people it was easy to organise sports teams, debating competitions—whatever you wanted. I didn't know everyone on the course by any means but I made many new friends.

*Teaching and Facilities*

Every institution will teach the BPTC using slightly different methods in very different facilities. You may want to ask the following:

- How much teaching is done in small groups and what size are the groups?

- Where does the advocacy tuition take place? Will you be taught in a classroom or does the course have the use of a mock courtroom for added realism?

- Will all your advocacy exercises be recorded so you can watch them yourself?

- Which options are offered? Is there an option in the area you want to practise?

- What pro bono opportunities are there? Is there a student-run legal advice centre?

- Are there mooting competitions?

- Are there student societies and sports teams?

- Would it be possible to set up your own student society? How much support would you be given?

*How is the Course Assessed?*

Some providers now give law degree graduates the opportunity to "upgrade" a BPTC qualification to an LLM in Legal Practice. This is unlikely to impress pupillage committees who should be wise to the upgrade system but may be useful if you wish to practise overseas. If this is an attractive option, contact the providers for further information.

*Where do You Want to do Pupillage?*

Doing the BPTC is an excellent way of meeting practitioners. Often, parts of the course will be taught by barristers practising locally. If you can get to know these barristers on the BPTC and impress them there, you may be at an advantage if you subsequently apply to their chambers for a pupillage.

If you know that you want to apply for pupillage and practise outside London, it can be a good idea to apply for the BPTC in that region (if it is offered). Although by no means essential, this can show a commitment to a city or area that some pupillage committees like to see: it will be easier to persuade chambers that you are not planning to take up their time getting qualified and then leave to go somewhere else.

When I was applying for pupillage, my chambers was impressed I'd studied in Leeds: it showed I had a link to the area.

*Leila Benyounes, Park Lane Plowden, Leeds*

*A former BVC Student (Newcastle)*
I couldn't afford the BVC in London. I knew I wanted to practise in Newcastle so I decided to go there for the BVC. It was a lot cheaper. The

great thing was that the teaching staff on the BVC was largely made up of experienced barristers, many of whom still practised on the North-East circuit. The North-East circuit is very friendly and I found my BVC year a great time to network and make contacts at the local Bar.

*The City*

Finally, consider the city itself. You will not spend your entire time reading books and practising your advocacy. What is the nightlife like? What is the culture like? Will you feel at home there?

**Applications**

The only way to apply for the BPTC is through the website *www.bptconline.co.uk*. This is a central system for all providers: you cannot apply directly to the providers themselves. You must submit your applications (and pay an administrative charge) on this website before mid-January of the year you wish to start the BPTC. Check the website for the exact deadline each year.

**Making the Most of the BPTC**

Having invested so much in the course, you should approach your studies with the determination to maximise all opportunities that present themselves.

I hear people saying that it's possible to survive the BPTC just by turning up to the minimum number of classes and doing a bit of cramming before the exams. In a sense this is right: some students do manage to complete the course without really applying themselves to their studies. But what these people ignore is that the BPTC is not like other, academic, courses. A good result in the Bar exams is not the only goal of the BPTC. To think this way is to approach the course with entirely the wrong mindset.

In simple terms, the BPTC is not about the BPTC. It is about becoming an outstanding advocate.

Every year I see students who realise this fact. If they scored 50 per cent on a piece of drafting, they go away and do it again in their own time, so that they score 70 per cent. When they score 70 per cent, they go away and do it again in their own time so that they score 90 per cent. They watch the recordings of their advocacy several times over and repeat them several times, each time ironing out a small fault, each time becoming better advocates.

Of course, these things can seem overly eager. And they don't fit the 'do the bare minimum to survive' attitude to studies that some students have. But, year after year, it is these eager students who win the mooting competitions, who find offers of pupillage and who go on to fight like lions for their clients. And this last, surely, is what being a barrister is all about.

So is it an easy year? It can be—if you want it to be. But if you have the drive to care about achieving your potential—and doing your best for future clients—it is anything but.

*James Wakefield, Bar Course Director, Kaplan Law School*

*Advocacy*

Chief among these opportunities is the chance to develop as an advocate. Most of your teachers on the BPTC will have experience of being practising barristers and some will continue to practise. They are therefore in an excellent position to teach you exactly those skills you will need for the first few years of practice and, crucially, for pupillage interviews. The sensible student will take the advocacy training seriously.

**Making the Most of Advocacy Classes**

1. Feedback
Feedback is essential for improvement. Do not take it personally; embrace it as a way to get better. Your tutor should give you specific points of feedback. Be sure to note down the points they make very carefully. But do not stop there. Remember that being an advocate is about appealing to as many different people as possible. Ask what the other members of your group thought. They may have spotted something—a habit or mannerism—that your tutor missed. Once you have a list of points to improve, think carefully about how you are going to make the necessary changes.

2. Self-criticism
Feedback from others is very important, but another good way of understanding your limitations as an advocate is to watch and listen to yourself.

Many people think they sound like Rumpole of the Bailey and will ignore all criticism of themselves. It is not until they see a video that they understand that they really do say "Umm" every third word and that their hands fidget in a very distracting manner. Record your advocacy sessions and review them carefully afterwards. At first it will feel strange (and probably very embarrassing) to watch yourself. Do not let this put you off!

### 3. Practice

Once you have identified where you went wrong, do not miss the final stage of improvement. Go back and do the piece of advocacy again. Watch it again, paying particular attention to the problems you identified, and see if you have improved. If you have not, do it again.

> There is a real danger of being pompous. We all deserve to be brought down a peg or two as frequently as possible.
>
> *Miles Copeland, Three New Square*

> Most people who encounter problems on the BPTC do so because of poor time-management. Try to approach the BPTC as the first year of your professional life. It is a rigorous course—but you are training to become a barrister.
>
> *Nicki McLaren, Course Leader at BPP London*

> The Bar is all about research and advocacy. Concentrate on improving these skills on the BPTC so that you have the skills to take any work that comes in when you get to Chambers.
>
> *Stephen Migdal, Course Leader at UWE*

*Assessments*

There are four different grades: Outstanding, Very Competent, Competent and Not Competent. You should be aiming for one of the first two.

As with all assessments, one of the most important ways to prepare is to know how they are marked. Your BPTC provider will be required to provide you with a list of assessment criteria for each subject. Pay careful attention to these.

Do not make the common mistake of underestimating the multiple choice exams. Revise carefully. When you are answering the questions, be sure to read through all the options before you make your choice: two or more of the options can be very similar.

*Former BVC Student*

Multiple choice tests? Pah! I thought if I've written a thesis on employment law then 'multiguess' would be entirely straightforward. The right answer was after all guaranteed to be there in front of me—all I had to do is recognise it.

It turned out I was in for a bit of a shock. These were the hardest exams on the course. The four options were always very similar and all seemed entirely plausible. More often than not I'd read the first option and be sure that was right. Then I'd read the second and third options and suddenly lose all confidence. Often the last option would be a combination of the first three! To revise properly you really have to learn the detail with precision. I messed up my mocks but worked harder for the final exams and thankfully did fine.

*Extra-Curricular*

Finally, be sure to do as many extra-curricular activities as you possibly can. See Chapter 16 for which extra activities will strengthen your pupillage application and how to get involved in them.

**Details of the Providers**

*Provider: BPP*
Part-time option: Yes
Number of students per year: 250 FT and 100 PT London; 50 FT and 50 PT Leeds
Location: London and Leeds
Contact: Emma Hammond—emmahammond@bppls.com
Website: *www.bpp.com/law*

*Provider: Cardiff University*
Part-time option: No
Number of students per year: 60
Location: Cardiff

Contact: Hannah Walsh—walshhj@cardiff.ac.uk
Website: *www.law.cf.ac.uk/cpls*

*Provider: College of Law*
Part-time option: Yes
Number of students per year: 250 FT and 50 PT London; 65 FT Birmingham
Location: London and Birmingham (full-time only)
Contact: Sue Drury—susan-drury@lawcol.co.uk
Website: *www.college-of-law.co.uk*

*Provider: Inns of Court School of Law*
Part-time option: Yes
Number of students per year: 500 FT and 50 PT
Location: London
Contact: Carol Gould—c.gould@city.ac.uk
Website: *www.city.ac.uk/law*

*Provider: Manchester Metropolitan University*
Part-time option: Yes
Number of students per year: 110
Location: Manchester
Contact: Wanda Clarke—w.clark@mmu.ac.uk
Website: *www.law.mmu.ac.uk/postgrad*

*Provider: Northumbria University*
Part-time option: Yes
Number of students per year: 80 FT and 20 LLB Exempting Degree
Location: Newcastle-upon-Tyne
Contact: Dawn Haynes—dawn.haynes@unn.ac.uk
Website: *http://northumbria.ac.uk/sd/academic/law/postgradprof*

*Provider: Nottingham Law School*
Part-time option: No
Number of students per year: 120
Location: Nottingham
Contact: Viv Beaumont—viv.beaumont@ntu.ac.uk
Website: *www.ntu.ac.uk/nls/professional-courses/BPTC*

*Provider: Kaplan Law School (from 2010)*
Part-time option: No
Number of students per year: 60
Location: London
Contact: info@kaplanlawschool.org.uk
Website: *www.kaplanlawschool.org.uk/Qualifications/BVC/tabid/78/Default.aspx*

*Provider: University of the West of England*
Part-time option: Yes
Number of students per year: 120 FT and 40 PT
Location: Bristol
Contact: Gillian Burridge—gillian.burridge@uwe.ac.uk
Website: *http://bilp.uwe.ac.uk*

# SECTION 4: GAINING EXPERIENCE AND DEVELOPING YOUR TALENTS

Distinguish yourself from the crowd. There are a very, very great number of applicants for a finite number of placements. One way to distinguish yourself is by having an outstanding academic record. But this is not the only way. Another way is to have relevant experience of practice in the law and to be able to speak thoughtfully and intelligently about those experiences.

*Richard Wald, 39 Essex Street*

It's really important to show you have outside interests. We get forms filled with academic information and lists of prizes but we get no sense at all of what these people are like. We don't want someone who has spent all of university in the corner of the library; they won't be a good barrister—they won't have the interpersonal skills.

*Susannah Jones, 20 Essex Street*

Try to come across as original and different—it's very, very difficult to stand out from the crowd. When we are getting 200–300 applications, all of which are very good, you do need something so that when you are application 150 or 151 in the pile, you are more than just a number. Try to make your CV sing by doing something different.

*Gwion Lewis, Landmark Chambers*

To reach a pupillage interview, your application will have to survive rigorous assessment by chambers' pupillage committees. While style and tone are important, most important of all is content. In order to have a CV that can stand up to the scrutiny of a pupillage committee, you will have to spend a considerable amount of time doing legal and non-legal work experience and activities. You will need mini-pupillages, advocacy experience such as mooting and debating, work experience and outside interests.

Beyond bolstering your CV, such activities can be hugely enjoyable and rewarding.

# 11 MINI-PUPILLAGES

For those considering a careeer at the Bar I would say investigate it in as much detail as you can. Consider doing mini-pupillages and ask as many questions as possible. Once you have a clear idea what it's all about and if you are still keen on becoming a barrister and think you can make it then I would say go for it. It really is an incredible profession and a great privilege to be a part of.

*Tim Kevan, barrister and author of*
BabyBarista and the Art of War (*Bloomsbury 2009*)

## Mini-Pupillages: An Overview

*What is a Mini-Pupillage?*

A mini-pupillage, or "mini", is the name given to a short period of time spent undertaking work experience in barristers' chambers. Occasionally minis are paid and highly structured with a group of mini-pupils receiving talks from members of chambers and attending court in groups. These, however, are rare; most minis will be both unfunded and unstructured. You are likely to be the only mini-pupil in chambers that week and you will probably be assigned to a different barrister each day, sometimes at the last minute, depending on who is available. Some minis are also assessed, usually meaning you will be given a piece of work to do over the course of the week.

Experiences can be glamorous and exciting—discussing cross-examination strategy with a QC in a high profile case then watching as it is put into devastating effect—or mundane and uninspiring—sitting at the back of a hot courtroom day after day watching a boring case and having no interaction with anybody. Most often, your experience will be somewhere between these two extremes. You will probably find yourself reading briefs and discussing them with a barrister, sitting in on a client conference or two and perhaps being invited to lunch so you can meet members of chambers. Whatever your experience, one thing is always guaranteed: you will learn something about practice at the Bar.

*A Former Mini-Pupil*

I did one mini where every single case I went to watch settled. Chambers was keen to remind me that this was far from the general reality of their practice. At first I was disappointed not to see the barristers on their feet because this is what I had come to see. However I soon realised that I was getting a crash course in negotiation, addressing clients' expectations and dealing with Counsel on the other side. It certainly showed me an important part of practice that I hadn't really considered before. It taught me that every day at the Bar can be different: one minute you may be preparing to walk into an exciting case and the next you are spending the afternoon in a conference room hammering out the details of a settlement. The experience gave me lots to talk about at interview.

## Why Are They Important?

Mini-pupillages are the closest you can get to experiencing life at the Bar without actually being a barrister. They show you how barristers interact with solicitors, with lay clients and with other barristers. You will see what it means to be self-employed. You will also get a flavour of the atmosphere in different sets of chambers. All of this is invaluable—both for deciding whether to be a barrister and for choosing the area you want to practise.

Another reason to do mini-pupillages is that they can be excellent groundwork for subsequent pupillage applications. Chambers generally offer more minis than pupillage interviews, so statistically you are more likely to be invited for a mini than for an interview for pupillage. Once you are inside chambers you have the opportunity to demonstrate your strength as a pupillage candidate. You will almost certainly spend some time with a member of the pupillage interview panel (although you may not be told this) and if you can impress them with your interpersonal skills or your response to a problem question, you can put yourself at a significant advantage. Your name may even be passed on to the pupillage committee with a recommendation. So long as you don't submit a hopelessly weak pupillage application form, a good mini can sometimes get you to the first round of interviews. Remember, however, that this level of exposure works both ways. If you make a bad impression by turning up late or inappropriately giving a client legal advice, you are likely to find yourself on the receiving end of a short "application unsuccessful" letter if you later apply for pupillage.

Your behaviour on a mini is important. Don't get too relaxed. Whatever you do, don't (as one mini-pupil we had did) bring out a Game Boy . . .

*Barney Branston, 5 Essex Court*

## *How Many Should I Do?*

According to the Bar Council, 32.9 per cent of BVC students surveyed had undertaken either one mini or no minis at all. Even taking into account students who have no intention of practising in England and Wales, this figure is disappointingly high. Pupillage committees seek candidates who can demonstrate a commitment to the Bar. Precisely how many mini-pupillages it takes to demonstrate such a commitment is impossible to say, but it is generally agreed that you should be aiming for at least three. Different barristers will give you different advice about an optimum number. Some will advocate doing as many as possible while others will say that a stack of minis on your OLPAS form will scream to them that you haven't been using your time wisely. Use your common sense: ensure you've had experience at a few different types of set and seen a few different areas of law, possibly both in London and the provinces. If you want to do more, do so. If you feel you've done enough, and can justify this to an interviewing panel, then stop.

**Note:** Because of the nature of a barrister's work, you may have to travel to watch your mini-pupil supervisor in court. Travel expenses are unlikely to be reimbursed. If you are on a tight budget, inform the mini-pupillage coordinator before you arrive and they may be able to send you to something closer.

## Mini-Minis

*A Pupil*

As a single mother of two, it was very difficult for me to fit in a number of week-long minis around my commitments at home. When I was applying for minis, I explained my situation to chambers and asked if it would be possible to visit chambers for just one or two days instead of the whole week. Everyone was very kind and accommodating and I was able to arrange 'mini-minis' which were excellent.

## Applying for Mini-Pupillages

*Competition*

The competition for minis, though less extreme than for pupillage, can be intense. Chambers can get hundreds of applications for just a few places. Do not underestimate this competition: take the time to ensure that your application is as strong as possible.

At most chambers the application process consists of sending a CV and covering letter to the barrister in charge of mini-pupillages. At others there is a mini-pupillage application form and sometimes even an interview. Some chambers adopt a policy of selecting not on merit but entirely at random. Check each chambers' website for details.

*When to Apply*

Some chambers accept mini-pupillage applications all year round; others have strict deadlines. It is essential to spend a few hours researching chambers in the fields which interest you, either on the internet or by reading a pupillage guide. Note down their application deadlines in your diary. As the academic year progresses, competition for minis increases as students suddenly notice gaps in their CVs. If you can submit your applications early, you may be able to beat the rush and thereby maximise your chances of success. If you are asked to suggest dates you are available, try to offer as many as possible. Be aware that minis during reading weeks and holiday periods become fully booked very quickly.

> **One Chambers, One Mini: Choose Your Time Wisely:** There is so much competition for minis that the same person will rarely be invited twice. Be intelligent in timing your minis. If you have a first-choice chambers, schedule your mini for the time when you will be most impressive, particularly if the mini will be assessed. Wait until you have a couple of other minis behind you and you know something about legal practice and the Bar. With more experience, you should be more likely to impress.

*What to Write in an Application Letter*

There are two crucial questions that your mini-pupillage application to chambers needs to address: why you have applied to them and why they should choose you. You need to explain in detail why that particular chambers interests you. It could be the wide range of civil work that they do, the excellent reputation they have for human rights or because you were impressed by one of their barristers in court. See Chapter 21 for ideas on how to address this question more fully. Whatever your reason, make sure that you have done your research thoroughly. They will not be impressed if you focus on their family expertise when they only have a small practice in this area and their true speciality is in crime. Also be sure that the reason you offer is specific to that set: a standardised letter is not just wholly unimpressive, it can seem lazy or even rude.

When you have addressed the first question, you then need to promote yourself and explain why you are the best candidate for the mini-pupillage. As modestly as possible, sing your own praises. Tell them about the scholarship you won, the competition in which you did well or the moot that you entered. Tell them why you like their area of law. Finally, remember to say when you are available and sign the letter correctly with "Yours sincerely" (since your letter should be addressed to a named person). And then stop before the letter goes over a page.

## Rejections

If you find that you are getting rejections, show your applications to a careers adviser, tutor, friend or colleague. Your lack of success could be caused by something as simple as spelling the set's name incorrectly, getting your own telephone number wrong or inadvertently omitting some undergraduate degree marks from your CV. If you have friends who have been offered several minis, you may want to ask them if they could look over one of your application letters or if they could give you any tips.

### A Successful Mini-Pupillage Applicant
After getting a couple of rejection letters, I took my mini-pupillage applications to my Director of Studies. He made a few changes such as adding my part-time summer jobs and taking out my irrelevant non-legal work experience. It seemed fairly insignificant but it made a huge difference and afterwards I was offered more mini-pupillages than I had time to do.

If you still don't have any success after this, think about the quality of chambers to which you are applying. Instead of applying to the leading property set, for example, perhaps you should start lower and aim for somewhere less high-profile. You can always apply again to the leading set when you have more experience.

## On the Mini

*How to Make a Good Impression*

The ideal mini-pupil engages with what is going on around him but is also able to keep a low profile and fade into the wallpaper when required to do so. Barristers want you to ask questions: this demonstrates that you are thinking about what you are seeing and, ultimately, learning. However, you need to choose your time carefully. Save your questions and observations for a break or the end of the day when the client is not present. Remember: the client is paying for the barrister's undivided attention and not your thoughts.

A mini-pupil who interrupts at court or in a conference is a disaster, particularly if they contradict you.

*Richard Sear, 1 Hare Court*

If you are going to court, the ability to blend into the background is vital. Just before court I need to be concentrating on the client so it's a question of saving questions until after court or the train journey home.

The best advice for mini-pupils is to keep your eyes and ears open and engage in the experience. In this way you will get the most out of it.

*Jennie Gillies, 4 Pump Court*

**Mini-Tip:** If you are in court or sitting in on a conference, ask yourself what you think about the case. Do you think that the client has a strong chance of success? If in court, what do you think of the opposing Counsel's advocacy? Is there some element of the law unfolding that you find interesting, and if so why? It is very likely that the barrister will ask you what you think about what you have seen. He will be more impressed if you can give a specific answer or raise a pertinent question than if you reply with a standard "it's really interesting".

**A Word of Advice about "Networking"**

Networking is often misunderstood and tarnished with unpleasant associations. There are two kinds. One is networking for information. The other is networking to get a job. The first can be a step towards the second, but it is different, wholly acceptable if done tactfully, and invaluable. Do it.

Most members of the Bar are genuinely pleased if a bright person shows an interest in their career. Ask open but intelligent questions: 'When you started out what did you find the steepest learning curve?' 'How do you manage the hectic lifestyle?' Even better, try to tie your questions to evidence that you have read about an issue: '*The Times* last week said that the future of the publicly funded Bar is hanging by a thread. Do you think that's true?'

Mini-pupillages give you a great opportunity to practise overcoming any natural shyness you feel when it comes to making personal contacts. If you hate presenting yourself to strangers and then engaging them in conversation, think very carefully about whether you are suited to the Bar. It is a networking profession.

*Dr Ruth Smith, Cambridge University Careers Service*

*The Assessed Mini-Pupillage*

The assessed mini-pupillage is used by chambers either to scout out the top candidates before receiving the flood of pupillage application forms or, increasingly, as a formal and substantive part of the pupillage application process itself. It is effectively a form of extended interview. You should approach this as an opportunity to impress rather than a reason to be nervous.

The major difference with an assessed mini is that you will usually be given a problem question to work on. This may be a hypothetical academic question of law or an issue arising from a case in which chambers has recently been involved. After researching the point you will be asked to present your answer—on paper, orally or both. Although you will probably be given time to work on the problem during the day, you should not be surprised if you need to supplement this by spending time on it in the evenings. Either way, ensure that you take the task seriously and work hard on your answer. Your work should be presented clearly and reasoned logically: you can expect that your analysis and conclusions will be scrutinised by some very experienced people who will not be shy about challenging you. For more detail about how to answer legal problem questions successfully, see Chapter 22 on interviews.

When you are writing up a problem question, insert paragraph numbers. Everyone in chambers always uses paragraph numbers and mini-pupils never do but it can make their work look much more professional.

*Susannah Jones, 20 Essex Street*

On an assessed mini, remember that it is likely that your week's performance will be filed and referred to when your pupillage application reaches chambers.

**Mini-Pupillage Etiquette:** There are unwritten rules of mini-pupillages which you may only discover by inadvertently breaking:

- Dress correctly. Wear a dark suit. If you are inappropriately dressed, chambers will not be able to send you to court or to attend anything where client contact is involved. Ladies, if you are wearing a skirt, make sure that it is not too short—around knee length is acceptable—do not wear anything low cut and always wear tights. Gentlemen, if you normally shave, remember to do so.

- Turn your phone off. There are few things more embarrassing than your mobile ringing in a conference with a client or, worse, in court. It looks wholly unprofessional.

- Arrive on time. You will often be asked to arrive before court starts so that the barrister appearing can brief you on the case. If you are late you may miss this opportunity and, worse, irritate the barrister. Sometimes you will be told to meet the barrister at court. Make sure that you are clear which court (not only the address but the courtroom itself), where it is and how long it takes to get there. Do not be afraid to ask the clerks for this information if you are unsure.

- Be cautious about offering a handshake when meeting barristers. Historically barristers did not shake hands with each other and some barristers maintain this tradition.

- Never speak in court or in conferences with clients—not even if you think that you have thought of the knockout argument that will win the case or if you have a witty little anecdote that shows that you fully understand the client's predicament. As with every cast-iron rule there is an exception: you can speak when spoken to.

- Don't fall asleep in court. Obvious but not unheard of . . .

**Mini-Tip:** Take a book (and the sort of book that you will not be embarrassed to be seen reading). You may have to go by train to meet a barrister in a far-flung court or spend most of your first morning sitting in the waiting room.

## After a Mini

Pupillage application forms often ask what you learnt on your work experience. In preparation, it is therefore a good idea to make notes of everything that you experienced during your mini.

Consider all the things you actually learnt and be specific. If you learnt that preparation is paramount and can win you the case, write about it. If you learnt that the reality of practice involves a lot of travel and waiting outside courts but you saw that this time can be put to good use, say so. Chambers will want to know you understand what you are taking on and that you will not be disillusioned and quit after they offer you pupillage or tenancy. Write such lists shortly after you complete the mini-pupillage while everything is still fresh in your head.

This technique can also be applied to other work experience.

### Example of Notes from a Mini-Pupillage:

Mini-pupillage with Fictional Chambers:

- Spoke to head of chambers about his practice (planning law).
- Attended a planning inquiry.
- Went on a site visit.
- Sat in on a client conference.
- Talked to a barrister about the book he is updating on planning guidelines.

What I learnt:

- I began to gain an understanding of the practice of planning law in particular how it involves [an example].
- I learnt the procedure for a planning inquiry and the importance of discussing this procedure with the client and ensuring that they fully understand it.

- I learnt the significance of site visits to a practice in planning law and how essential it is to double check the documentary information which is provided.

- I began to learn the importance of pre-conference preparation and how to manage a client's expectations in a conference.

Keep these lists somewhere safe and refer to them when the time comes to complete your pupillage applications. They will save you a great deal of time and effort.

**Tip:** As a mini-pupil you are taking up professional time. Remember to thank chambers and individual supervisors. A thank you letter might be a good idea.

# 12 MOOTING

*by Joseph Sullivan, 2 Temple Gardens, winner of the Rosamund Smith Middle Temple Mooting Competition*

> Try and do as much mooting as possible: the only way to get good at arguing cases is by practising.
>
> *Nicholas McBride, Director of Studies in Law at Pembroke College, Cambridge, and author of* Letters to a Law Student

## What is a Moot?

A moot is a competition in which competitors act as the advocates arguing a legal dispute as if in court. The case to be argued is given to them in advance (normally at least a week before the moot). Moots are based purely on one or more points of law: the facts provided cannot be disputed. A moot problem usually takes the form of an appeal from an earlier (fictional) court decision.

The aim for each advocate, as in real-life litigation, is to persuade the judge that his case is stronger than his opponent's.

There are two teams, each consisting of two people. Each team is usually judged as a team but, depending on the rules of the competition, team members may be judged individually. The pair arguing that the previous decision should be reversed is called the "Appellant", whilst the team seeking to uphold the decision is called the "Respondent". At some pre-arranged time before the moot, each team must provide the other team and the judge with a "Skeleton Argument". This is a short document, akin to those used in real-life litigation, which outlines the team's case. Typically, on the day of the moot, each team must also provide a printed copy of each case upon which they rely, known as their "bundle".

At the moot itself, each participant will have a prescribed amount of time (usually 15 minutes) to present arguments, "submissions", orally to the judge. The first speaker for the Appellant, the "Senior Appellant", begins and is ordinarily followed by the "Senior Respondent", then the "Junior Appellant" and finally the "Junior Respondent" but this order can vary between competitions. Note that the Senior and Junior positions are not reflective of either the ability of the advocates or the difficulty of the point of law. In some competitions there may be a "right of reply" given to the Appellant. This is a short period of time (around five minutes) given to allow the Appellant to respond to any new points made by the Respondent. During the course of all of the submissions, the judge can intervene to ask questions. Unlike debating, competitors must never interrupt another speaker.

After the submissions are completed, the judge gives a judgment on the law, i.e. he says whether the appeal was successful. Then, most importantly, the judge decides which team won the moot itself, based on their overall performance; the winning team will not necessarily be the team which won on the law.

## Why Should You Moot?

Perhaps the most cynical motivation to moot is that it will look good on your CV. The reason it will look good on your CV however reveals the real rationale for why you should moot. Mooting helps to develop many of the key skills necessary for a career at the Bar. The preparation required involves legal research and careful analysis of the problem before you. To be successful you must think creatively about the problem to decide the best angle of attack.

Oral advocacy is the skill most obviously developed by mooting. There is no substitute for standing up and presenting legal arguments to a judge. Experience of mooting suggests to chambers that an applicant for pupillage can articulately present legal submissions and has the speed of thought necessary to deal with a judge's questions.

> I learnt more about advocacy from taking part in an Inn mooting competition than I learnt on the whole of the BVC.
>
> *Richard Sear, 1 Hare Court*

## Marking Criteria

Many mooters spend so much time preparing their legal arguments that they lose sight of how they will be scored. You must strike a balance: clearly explain the reasoning supporting your legal position but also think about how to be a persuasive advocate. Expect your opponents to have solid legal arguments—you must offer more than mere analysis if you are to win the moot.

Each competition should have its own marking criteria stated within the rules; however, judges should take into account the following factors, which should be kept in mind at all stages of preparation and delivery:

- Quality of skeleton arguments.

- Reference to skeleton arguments in the course of submissions.

- Strength of legal reasoning.

- Ingenuity of submissions.

- Clarity of speech.

- Visual presentation (i.e. good posture and keeping still).

- Ability to respond to judicial questioning.

- Flexibility of submissions (i.e. the ability to adapt to intervention).

- Eye contact.

- Teamwork.

- Use of proper court-room language.

## Creating and Developing Arguments: Making a Persuasive Case

*Step 1*—Read the moot problem carefully several times. Check which court the moot will be set in: anywhere lower than the Supreme Court and there may be binding precedent to contend with (remember that the Court of Appeal binds itself). In the Supreme Court there is never binding domestic precedent but authorities are still persuasive and it is imperative that you use them.

> **Tip:** Be clear in your mind precisely what conclusion you want the judge to come to. Some people find it helpful to write this down before they begin their research.

*Step 2*—If the problem mentions two specific grounds of appeal, decide how to allocate them between you (by convention the Senior usually takes the first point). If there is only one specified ground of appeal (or none at all), keep this in mind as you conduct your research and consider how you will divide the arguments between your speeches.

*Step 3*—If there are any cases cited in the problem read them thoroughly. Think about the similarities and differences between these cases and the moot problem.

*Step 4*—Go to the student and/or practitioner books in the relevant area of law. These will direct you to further pertinent case law and academic literature. Keyword searches on LexisNexis, Westlaw, Lawtel or other electronic legal databases are also useful at this stage. These can be accessed from the Inns' libraries. In addition, you should use these websites to ensure that the authorities you have read have not been overturned.

*Step 5*—Divide the authorities you have found into those which support your case and those which are unfavourable. Think about how you will persuade the judge that the authorities which support your case are analogous to the facts and legal issues arising in the moot problem.

*Step 6*—You cannot simply ignore those authorities which are unfavourable to your case. You must make a plan for how you will distinguish them. Distinguishing a previous case involves showing the judge that the rule therein ought not to be applied to the problem at hand. You need to show that there is some difference between the previous authority and the mooting problem and that this difference renders the reasoning used in the earlier authority inapplicable to your case.

*Step 7*—Try to anticipate how your opponents will seek to distinguish your authorities. If there are dissenting judgments then be prepared to deal with the reasoning therein, especially if your moot is before the Supreme Court.

*Step 8*—Discuss with your partner which authorities you will cite in your skeleton argument. Double-check that the cases you have chosen are the highest authorities available for the points you are trying to make and that the judgments/speeches you are relying on are those of the majority if from the Court of Appeal or the Supreme Court. If you do intend to rely upon the persuasive force of a dissenting judgment then be prepared for tough questions as to why the dissenter should be preferred to the majority.

*Step 9*—If the mooting problem raises a novel point of law, or is to be heard by the Supreme Court, then you are not confined to arguing from authority. Think about the policy reasons for and against the approach you are advocating. An academic article which supports your position can be useful here, though be careful not to cite one just for the sake of it.

## Skeleton Arguments

Your skeleton argument has three functions. First, it introduces the judge and your opponents to what you are going to say, allowing all parties to be fully prepared and ensuring there are no surprise cases cited or unexpected points made. Secondly, it helps the judge follow your oral submissions while you are on your feet. Finally, it helps the judge recall your submissions after you have sat down.

The secret to writing a successful skeleton argument lies in finding the right balance between lucidity and concision. A good skeleton should explain the points you are going to make and the cases you are going to cite in sufficient detail to fulfil the aims set out above. However, it should not be so long that it leaves no room for you to develop your arguments in your speech, nor should it be tiresome to read.

There is also a tactical element to consider: you must give the judge a clear outline of your case in order to maximise the time allowed for oral arguments whilst leaving enough flexibility to manoeuvre later. Your skeleton argument must never be wilfully misleading: everything must be accurate and you must intend it to form the basis of your oral submissions.

### How to Write a Winning Skeleton Argument

1. Research separately from your team-mate before you sit down together to discuss your strategy. This will result in more ideas for you to choose from when you eventually come to deciding which arguments to advance.

2. Make your best points first. This means that if you run out of time, you will at least have addressed the crucial areas in the moot.

3. Be flexible. When difficulties arise in the details, even if you have already drafted a skeleton argument, don't be afraid to start again taking a fresh approach.

4. Beware the common mistake of trying to fit too much into your skeleton argument. Rushed submissions seldom win a moot. When hours have been spent researching a problem it is very tempting to want to include everything you have uncovered, but you must be selective. Each mooter should try to avoid making more than three distinct arguments.

5. Ensure your skeleton argument is well spaced and that the paragraphs are numbered. Ideally, use headings and sub-headings. Layout and presentation are vital: you want the document to be as easy to read as possible. Type your name at the end and sign it.

## The Language of Mooting

In a moot there are certain rules about the language you may use and the way you must act, just as there are in real courtrooms.

The Senior Appellant must introduce all four mooters at the beginning of the moot before he begins his speech. He should then briefly outline his Junior's submissions as well as his own. The Senior Respondent should do the same. You must use proper courtroom language and no colloquialisms:

- Your fellow mooters should each be referred to as "My Learned Friend" (e.g. "My Learned Friend submitted that . . .").

- The first time a case is cited in the moot, its full name must be given along with a citation in its full form. Thereafter it may be referred to in a shorter form.

- The judge must be given his proper title depending on seniority ("My Lord" or "My Lady" and "Your Lordship" or "Your Ladyship" if sitting in the High Court or above).

- Express gratitude to the judge or Your Learned Friends by saying "I am obliged" or "I'm grateful". Avoid "thank you".

- If you are referring to a House of Lords case, remember that the judgments are referred to as "speeches".

- If you can see that you are running short of time, you can indicate this to the judge by saying "I am mindful of the time, my Lord".

- In criminal cases, refer to the parties in *R v Rogers* as *"The Crown and Rogers"*. In civil cases, *Davies v Rogers* would be referred to as *"Davies and Rogers"*.

- You must never say "In my opinion" or "I think". The safest option is to use "I submit" or "In my submission". The judge is not interested in your opinion: you are a conduit for your client's case.

**Preparing For Your Oral Submissions**

Do not write your speech out in full. Whilst it may be tempting to do so for security, the judge will notice and disapprove. You will not be demonstrating the essential skills of thinking on your feet and engaging your audience. In addition, judicial intervention can cause real problems when a mooter is reading out a pre-prepared speech because it is extremely difficult to be flexible. Instead of writing out your speech in full, make a list of the essential points you want to make and add some detail to these points.

Invariably, the rules will limit the number of authorities each team is allowed to cite (usually to three cases). However, it pays to be familiar with as much of the relevant case law as time permits, both to ensure that you cite the most appropriate cases available and because it is impressive if, in the event the judge refers to a case cited by neither team, you are able to deal with it knowledgably.

It is important that you read the opposing team's skeleton argument very carefully, together with their cited authorities in full. If your own skeleton does not fully address their arguments you must decide how you will deal with these in your speeches. Whilst you do not need to rebut everything the opposing team says, you must show that you have engaged with their submissions as this is one of the criteria the judge will mark you on.

To find an appropriate volume and speed, practise your submissions out loud and time them. Remember, you will need to speak more slowly than you would in normal conversation. If you can only just fit your submissions into the allotted time then they are too long—in the moot itself you will have to allow time for judicial intervention. Practise in front of your team-mate, then someone who has no prior knowledge of the legal problem you're dealing with. This will test the clarity of your submissions:

if someone who has not read the papers in advance can understand your arguments then it is likely that the judge will understand them.

For most moots you must provide the judge and the opposing team with your bundle of authorities. It is a good idea to enlarge photocopies to 120 per cent when you are copying law reports. This will make them easier for the judge to read and will remove any messy black space around the edge. While there is some disagreement on this point, you may wish to highlight the specific passages on which you intend to rely. This saves time in the moot and makes the judge's life easier. Ensure the bundle is paginated. Insert dividers between cases. Be aware that most mooters find putting together a good bundle a very time-consuming process.

**The Moot**

- Stand still whilst making your submissions. Try to keep hand movements to a minimum. Some advocates stand with their hands clasped behind them, some in front, others with their hands to their sides. Find the position which feels most comfortable for you and stick to it.

- Pay close attention to the other team's submissions, even if you have already made your own. It looks unprofessional to switch off after your part in the moot is complete.

- Take a stopwatch with you so you are not caught out by timing. In some moots the judge will not stop you once your time is up. This is not a licence to continue for as long as you like: exceeding the time limit will be taken into account when determining the winning team. In the event that the judge asks you a difficult question during the final minute of your speech, explain that you are aware of the time but continue to give a full answer. Timing is at the judge's discretion and you should not be penalised for addressing his question even if it takes you over time.

- Ensure your submissions have a coherent structure. It will assist the judge if this is the same as the structure in your skeleton argument. Begin your speech by briefly outlining all your submissions and enumerate them. Make regular reference to your skeleton throughout.

- Actively pursue marks for teamwork. Refer to each other's submissions. If you spot a flaw in the other team's arguments which your partner can highlight in his speech, write him a note.

- Be aware of the judge. Ensure that you speak at a steady pace so he has time to make a note. If he is still writing at the end of a submission, pause until he has finished before going on. Be sensitive to the judge's demeanour and remarks: if he is clearly unimpressed by a particular submission after you have explained its substance then finish it quickly and move on to the next.

- Never talk over the judge. As soon as he starts speaking, you must stop even if you are mid-sentence.

- Don't panic when the judge asks a difficult question. If you need a moment to think of your response, take one.

- If a judge asks a question which you intend to cover later in your submissions, you must decide whether to answer it immediately, or tell the judge that you'll address it in due course. The latter is certainly the easier option but if you can, do the former. It is more impressive for you to show that you can quickly adapt and modify the structure of your submissions in response to the judge. In your answer ensure you refer to the relevant part of your skeleton argument: this highlights both that you anticipated the issue and that you are adapting your intended structure.

**Above all**: Make sure that your desire to win does not lead you to forget that integrity and sportsmanship are paramount.

# 13 DEBATING

*by Alexander Deane, past winner of the World Debating*
*Championships and Middle Temple Barrister*

## Introduction

A debate is a controlled, formal argument. Debates are won and lost by teams, not by individuals.

Debating is very different from court appearances—but participation (and, preferably, success!) is highly valued by pupillage committees as a demonstration of an interest and ability in advocacy. Debating experience can also be excellent preparation for pupillage interviews where you will often be asked to argue a topic with little or no preparation.

There are several different types of debating. In the UK, the most common is British Parliamentary (BP). This features eight speakers to a debate: on each side there are two teams of two speakers. Positions are randomly allocated which often leads to speaking in favour of things you don't believe in and against those that you do.

It is a subtle art involving not only competing jointly to beat the opposition but also competing with the other team on your side, without appearing to disagree with them.

## Judges and Debaters

The seating around the debating table is arranged as follows:

| JUDGE(S) | | | | |
|---|---|---|---|---|
| | PROPOSITION | | OPPOSITION | |
| 1st<br><br>T<br>E<br>A<br>M | First Proposition, Speaks first (Prime Minister) | | First Opposition, Speaks second (Leader of the Opposition) | 1st<br><br>T<br>E<br>A<br>M |
| | First Proposition, Speaks third (Deputy Prime Minister) | T<br>A<br>B<br>L<br>E | First Opposition, Speaks fourth (Deputy Leader of the Opposition) | |
| 2nd<br><br>T<br>E<br>A<br>M | Second Proposition, Speaks fifth (Member of Government) | | Second Opposition, Speaks sixth (Member of Opposition) | 2nd<br><br>T<br>E<br>A<br>M |
| | Second Proposition, Speaks seventh (The Government Whip) Final speaker for the Proposition | | Second Opposition, Speaks eighth (The Opposition Whip) Final speaker for the Opposition | |

There will be between one and five judges, who will be led by a "chairman". The chairman may be called Mr/Madam Speaker, Mr/Madam Chairman or Mr/Madam Chair.

Other speakers may be referred to by their position (e.g. Second Opposition), their role (e.g. Deputy Prime Minister), by their first name or by their last name—it really doesn't matter. Don't call people "the honourable". They're not. Similarly, do not call people "my learned friend"—an easy mistake to make if you are an experienced mooter.

After the debate, the judge(s) deliberate, and a decision is reached with all judges having an equal vote (this is different from other debating formats, where the judges may vote on a result without conferring). The chairman controls and directs the discussion. This discussion always aims for unanimity: if impossible, then a majority is sought. If a majority cannot be reached, then the chairman decides.

## How to Debate

*Before the Debate*

Generally, the topic is announced just 15 minutes prior to the debate itself. The subject of the debate is called the "motion" and is expressed in the format "This House . . ." followed by a statement of belief or will, which the Proposition teams will support and the Opposition teams oppose. Examples of motions include: "This House would legalise euthanasia" or "This House believes that the Olympic ideal is dead". Sometimes motions can be "open" in which case First Proposition can define them as they wish, for example "This House would wait and see".

**Using your Preparation Time Effectively:** Each team of two prepares by itself.

- Plan what you're going to say: what are your arguments?

- Attempt to predict what your opponents will say: how will they oppose ("rebut") your arguments?

- Plan your response to their rebuttal: how will you rebut the rebuttal?

- Which points for your team will be delivered by you and which by your partner?

- How will your speech be structured?

*Teamwork*

Debating is a team sport. Plenty of individuals speak very well and their team still loses. There's no point blaming your partner: you win or lose as a team.

You should tell your partner what you're going to say in a debate if you're speaking first and your speech should be shaped by the knowledge of what your partner will say. If you're speaking second, your plan for your speech should be shaped in the knowledge of what your partner is going to say and then in the debate it should be reshaped in light of what is actually said. Never walk into a debate with a partner who says "just back me up". You both have a responsibility to ensure that each understands the points the other will give. You should talk a lot to your partner before the debate, and write notes to one another during the debate as things change, noting new lines of argument and agreeing responses.

If you have a good point, you shouldn't think "this is my point, I'm making it". You should decide with your partner in which speech it will be most effective. Very often, speakers deliver good arguments well but are marked down because the argument is in the wrong place. Big, principled arguments belong in the first speech of each pair. This is logical: in the first half of the debate the first speaker sets out the key arguments and in the second half the summary speaker must not introduce new material.

*Speeches*

Speeches are five or seven minutes in length, depending on the competition. There is technically a grace period of 30 seconds after the end of the final minute, during which you may complete your speech. But be warned that you may be heavily penalised if you exceed the time limit even by as little as ten seconds.

Speakers' Roles and How the Debate Unfolds

The first speakers define their cases and deliver arguments for their teams. They also point to (flag) the points their partner will deliver.

All speakers except the first speaker for the Proposition have a responsibility to rebut (i.e. attack the arguments of) the speaker(s) who came before them on the other side. In particular, they have a specific responsibility to rebut the speaker who has spoken immediately before them. BP debating (unlike other kinds of debating, for instance those favoured in the United States) does not feature point-by-point judging, where each argument—no matter how trivial or stupid—must be rebutted. Your biggest responsibility is to knock down the other side's strongest arguments. There is less credit to be had for attacking the weak ones, but remember: the weaker the argument, the easier it should be to dismantle. Try to avoid leaving any points standing.

**First Proposition (First Prop)** The first speaker for the First Proposition (the Prime Minister) defines the motion and sets out the Proposition's line of argument (line) in the debate. Whilst there is no obligation to propose a practical method (policy) by which your argument would be implemented, debates are often poor if you don't and it is never wrong to deliver one.

**First Opposition (First Opp)** The First Opposition speaker sets out the opposition to the proposal by explaining the Opposition's line. Whilst First Proposition should have put forward a case with broad, contestable principles, it is down to First Opposition to show what the disagreement is between the two sides: to establish the "clash" in the debate.

One vital part of doing this is ensuring that you oppose the argument that is given, not merely the one you were expecting. First Opposition is the place where people are most often caught out—unprepared and unable to be versatile in the face of the unexpected. Listen to what First Prop says, then say why you disagree with it.

You can oppose the principle of the Proposition, the policy, or both. If opposing only the policy, you can recommend an alternative policy. Opposing on very narrow grounds (accepting most of what the Proposition says, and only opposing an element of it) is unwise. It can lead to a bad debate or a debate about very little, for which you will be blamed. Normally, defending the status quo is the right thing to do in opposition.

First Opposition, having set out the basis of his side's position, then delivers the main arguments for his team and flags the points his partner will make. It is not enough merely to define the Opposition line; he must also deliver substantive material for his side. Indeed, if a definition takes half the speech, it is too long.

The First Opposition speaker also rebuts the arguments advanced by First Proposition.

A frequent question is, should I challenge the Proposition's definition? A good rule of thumb is, don't do it. Debates about the definition of the debate are bad and horrible to watch—even the winners get low points. Normally, the definition is weak because the Proposition team is weak—so just beat them on the argument as they have framed it. Only the First Opposition speaker is allowed to challenge the motion. If they do not, the rest of the Opposition bench is bound by that decision.

**Seconding** Points allotted to the second speaker in the first speaker's speeches must be delivered: it is a serious teamwork flaw if an allotted point is promised by the first speaker and not delivered.

Seconders also rebut the material provided by the speaker(s) on the other side who have spoken before them. Speeches made in the second positions often give too much time to rebuttal and not enough to substantive material: though there are no hard and fast rules, if more than half a speech is spent rebutting, usually not enough time has been left for substantive arguments.

**Extending** Second Proposition or Opposition speakers on the table have an interesting job: to demonstrate that their team has something new to offer. Importantly, the second half of the table is not a new debate. The nature of the third speaker on each side of the table reflects the subtlety of the British format: material must be new but should not completely change the direction of the debate.

Third speaker approaches can take two forms: either new arguments and examples or a new analysis of arguments and examples that have already been delivered.

The second teams in BP debates must not contradict material set out by the first teams on their sides (not the principle, nor the policy, nor the examples, nor anything else). If done to a significant extent, it's called "knifing" and will greatly harm your team. It is difficult to beat a team on your side without contradicting them but that is part of the subtlety of the format. Teams going first will often try to deliver as much material as possible, starving the second teams of new ground—but they shouldn't make that overt. Similarly, teams in the second half of the debate will advance material that seeks to advance their side's position more effectively than the first team did; it may be chosen or flagged in a way that reveals faults in the first team's material, but those faults are not explicitly pointed out by the second team. Being on the same side is more than a formality: it has real meaning in the debate and though you're trying to beat the team alongside you, you must do this by being better, not by arguing against them.

**Summating** Final speakers offer a summary of the debate: they look back and say what happened. Think of a summary as a biased adjudication, highlighting the strengths of the winners (your side) and the weaknesses of the losers (the other side). Given this, whilst new examples are always welcome, summary speakers should never advance new arguments.

*Points of Information*

A point of information (PoI) is a question posed to a debater mid-argument. BP debating features no audience participation or judicial intervention. Opposing debaters may stand up and interject by offering a PoI (this is done by saying "On that point", "Point of information" or even simply "Sir!"). The speaker chooses whether to accept the point of information. If accepted, the debater offering the point may deliver it in a maximum of 15 seconds and sit down; if not accepted, he should sit down immediately. You may only offer PoIs to the opposing side of the table. PoIs cannot be offered in the first and last minute of a speech (protected time) where attempting to offer points is seen as bad manners. It is advisable to accept two PoIs during your speech and to offer at least two during each opposing speech.

PoIs are extremely important, they are the prime method of showing involvement throughout a debate and are one of the most obvious distinctions between debating and public speaking.

PoIs can be positive:

- Offering a new argument or example for your side.

- Highlighting an argument already delivered by your side that the opposition has ignored.

Or negative:

- Displaying inconsistency in an opposition speech or between speeches.

- Giving a fact or example that stands against their argument.

- Pointing out something they've got wrong.

## How to be Persuasive

*Structure*

Having a clear idea of what you're going to say helps the audience and helps you. A lack of structure damages more speeches than any other flaw. Basic errors in this area often lose debates simply because there isn't enough clarity in the delivery.

Structure should be easy to get right: say what you're going to say, say it in the order you've said you'll say it, and then say what you've said:

My three points are x y z.
X Y Z.
My three points were x y z.

Three is the magic number in debating: while it's not impossible to win
with two or four main points, three is effective for a strong speech.
Structuring a speech this way develops an involvement on the part of
listeners and an understanding of where the speaker is heading and what
they are trying to achieve.

### Reasons to Structure Your Speech

- Audiences feel most comfortable when they can easily follow a speaker. The
  delineation of one idea from another is helpful for listeners in both understanding and engaging with the argument.

- Complex ideas are most easily presented in a clear framework.

- You will find giving a speech easier when you have a clear idea of what
  you're going to say next—it will inform the point you develop before it, and
  diminish the possibility of confusion.

- Audiences and judges alike will accept swifter transition from one point to
  another (which might otherwise seem "clunky") if they know the next point
  is coming.

The selection of the three points, and the labels you give them, is more
important than it might appear. Even when the substance of a speech is
extremely good, the first three things most judges will have written down
on their marking sheets will be the three points you have promised. The
arguments you deliver should fit happily under those titles, and satisfy the
promise made by your label. If you promise a point, you or your team
must give it.

### *Style/Manner*

Debating is a persuasive art, not an essay-reading competition. Your
manner is important.
    Speed is a great problem. People often speak more quickly and lower
their volume when nervous. Don't mumble, but don't overcompensate
either—nobody enjoys being shouted at.

Avoid "ums" and "ers"; you'll find that slowing down helps as you'll start to be less worried about filling every second of silence. Indeed, pauses can be very effective. Use them. Beware of taking comfort in your notes. Reading is very irritating for the audience. Eye contact is important. To avoid sounding monotonous, vary the pitch of your voice as well as the speed.

## The Secrets of Future Success

1.  Your notes from past debates can be invaluable: they should be saved in a debating file. You'll often have a similar debate again in future competitions.

2.  Debating is hard work: if you want to be a serious, successful, competitive debater, you're going to have to hit the books. Because 15 minutes is not enough time to prepare speeches of very high quality, serious competitive debaters assemble files of material to bring to future debates. There are no rules preventing debaters bringing books or files to help them prepare their speeches. You will have to work at researching information and facts on current affairs, moral principles, basic legal rules, and so on.

3.  The most useful thing you can do to get better at debating is to debate more. Experience of the way a debate works, an instinct for what to say and when, and the confidence to advance a point under attack: these things come with time spent on your feet.

# 14 PRO BONO

Taken from the Latin term "pro bono publico" meaning "for the public good", pro bono is the name given to work that is done by a lawyer for free. There are opportunities for pro bono work throughout the legal profession and you will find practitioners of all levels who undertake pro bono work. There are even annual pro bono lawyers awards.

## The Free Representation Unit

Recommended by Tony Blair as being of "great benefit to both claimants and volunteer representatives", the Free Representation Unit ("FRU") is a charity which was established in 1972 by a small group of Bar students. FRU provides free legal representation in social security, employment and immigration cases to help those who would not otherwise receive any legal assistance.

Each year FRU trains 1,500 law students and professionals to work as representatives (reps). Training consists of a day of lectures given by practitioners and experienced FRU reps, followed by the independent writing of an opinion (two opinions for employment work) which is subsequently assessed. The final stage is a visit to a tribunal and the completion of a tribunal report. Following that, the rep is set loose on the public. Their work is carefully monitored by the full-time case-workers and an administrator on the FRU staff, all of whom offer help and support.

If you are interested in working for FRU it is best to sign up for a training day the moment you start law school as they are heavily over-subscribed. The Social Security Tribunal is probably the best place to start because, unlike employment, cases are rarely contested. This means that you will be making your arguments to a tribunal without an opponent. It is also common practice for submissions to be written. This is a far less nerve-wracking experience than oral submissions and excellent practice in written advocacy. The law is, in general, relatively straightforward and the cases can be extremely rewarding as you often encounter clients in terrible situations who greatly appreciate your help. Social security cases tend to take less time to complete and can therefore be fitted around full-time work or study more easily.

Employment work is tougher and you must either have completed the academic stage of training or be on the GDL in order to qualify as a rep. As well as being opposed, you will be required to make oral submissions and the law can be far more complicated.

> **A Word of Warning:** chambers are wise to applicants writing "FRU trained" on their applications. They know that this usually means the candidate has sat through a training day but has not actually tackled a case. It will not impress.

*A FRU Employment and Social Security Representative*
Taking on my first case within months of starting my legal education was a pretty daunting idea and I was terrified. I visited a tribunal as part of my training and watched a couple of cases, including one without representation. This had a huge impact on me. I began to appreciate, inexperienced as I was, that I would still have a great deal to offer a client.

A few weeks later, when I started working as a FRU Rep, I found that even before I started looking at the law I was able to help my clients in straightforward ways such as explaining to them what to expect. Tribunals, however friendly and sympathetic, will always seem frightening and intimidating. I found that simply by sitting with my clients on their side of the table and guiding them through, I was able to provide enormous support. You don't need to be a legal expert to do that. In fact, the law is quite straightforward for early cases and I received all the help I needed from the caseworker.

My advice to students considering FRU would be that even if you are only a couple of weeks into law school you can still make a huge difference to a client. Do not underestimate yourself.

*www.freerepresentationunit.org.uk*

## Citizens Advice Bureaux and Legal Advice Centres

Citizens Advice Bureaux (CAB) and Legal Advice Centres (LAC) provide an excellent chance to learn how to deal with clients and members of the public. Many law schools run their own legal advice clinics through which students can deal directly with clients and provide the legal advice themselves. This allows students to explore new areas of law as well as gaining valuable experience of client contact.

In high street CAB and LAC, law students are often taken on as volunteers in administrative roles while trained volunteers and qualified solicitors provide the advice. In exchange for your clerical skills you may be allowed to sit in on some conferences with clients.

*A CAB Volunteer*

I worked at a CAB one morning a week during my BVC year. Some days I would be filing and organising case notes while others I would be interviewing clients. You meet a very wide range of people, many with mental health problems—everyone from the genuinely aggrieved to the most vexatious of litigants. I gained experience dealing with really difficult people (I once had to call security) and I discovered the right balance between professionalism and compassion. It gave me my first contact with solicitors which will be crucial for building up my practice. Sitting in on conferences taught me how to talk to clients and guide them through the process of litigation from the very beginning. This meant I was in an excellent position for my conference exam on the BVC and I was asked about it in every pupillage interview.

At some centres, as well as the full-time caseworkers, solicitors from the major law firms volunteer on a monthly basis. This means you will get a chance to watch a variety of people at work with a variety of styles. You can witness ideas and techniques which you will then be able to adopt in your own practice.

You can approach your local CAB or LAC directly or try to get involved through your law school.

*www.citizensadvice.org.uk*

## Streetlaw

Streetlaw is a programme whereby students go into the community to talk about law. They visit such places as schools, prisons and youth centres and talk to audiences who usually have never considered a career in law and generally have given the subject of law itself little thought.

The aim is to talk about some legal issues that affect people's everyday lives—anything from the obvious (crime) to areas that are a little less publicised (for example how intellectual property rights affect nightclub DJs).

*A Streetlaw Volunteer*

I signed up and went to speak in an inner-city school in Nottingham. I took along various handouts and lesson plans I had carefully prepared for the sixth form general studies class I was going to be teaching.

The students weren't impressed with my pretty handouts showing members of society's rights and duties. In fact they weren't impressed with much apart from their phones and ipods. I could feel disaster looming . . .

I gave up on the plan pretty quickly and started to improvise. I reduced everything to fundamental questions about society and adapted it to be relevant to their lives. Slowly some students did start to come on board and express their views. As soon as a few had spoken, things snowballed and we had quite a lively debate.

I was a sweaty mess at the end of the class but it was quite enjoyable with hindsight. If you want to practise thinking on your feet and experiencing advocacy in a (very!) different forum from court I'd recommend it. After you've faced 24 teenagers, pupillage interviews are a lot less daunting!

Streetlaw is available through some law schools.

# 15 FURTHER LEGAL EXPERIENCE

> I don't recommend applying for pupillage until you are experienced enough in your area of interest to know it is what you want, and also to have the skills to impress chambers that you know what you are doing. A lot of applicants think you can get pupillage by blagging and bravado. In my experience those who get through tend to have done work of substance elsewhere and have coherent, compelling reasons why they want to practise at the Bar.
>
> *Afua Hirsch*, Guardian *Legal Affairs Correspondent*

Work experience and law-related experiences play a fundamental role as you begin your legal career. They give you insight into the practice of law and its effects on society. This will help you to decide which area of law to practise and confirm whether a legal career is, in fact, for you. Through such experience you can sample different aspects of legal and non-legal careers and develop skills which will be useful to discuss in interviews and to use when you start your practice.

## Short-Term Legal Activities and Experience

### Essay Prizes

Essay competitions run throughout the year and give you the opportunity to investigate an area of law while impressing chambers and even improving your bank balance. With the limited opportunities for independent research on the GDL, non-law graduates in particular may find that essay competitions are a useful way of researching topical areas of law. Even if you do not win the competition, you will have something interesting to discuss in a pupillage interview.

Competitions are run by several sources including chambers, the Inns and the legal press. Awards range from hundreds to thousands of pounds. Probably most famous is the annual One Essex Court Times Law Awards

Essay Competition. Appearing in *The Times* early each year, the competition invites essays of 1,000 words on a topic which has been in the legal headlines. It is possible to view the winning essays (and those of the runners up) on the One Essex Court website to give you an idea of what the judges are looking for. Although it takes valuable time, the competition is undoubtedly worth entering, with the winning entry published in *The Times* law section and scooping an impressive £3,500. The five other prize winners (selected from 12 finalists) are invited to an award dinner and win significant financial prizes.

Chambers often sponsor essay prizes through the law schools. This gives sets a chance to assess students before the pupillage applications begin. Essay competitions therefore give you an early opportunity to try to impress those chambers to which you might later wish to apply and winning a chambers' essay prize will almost certainly guarantee you a pupillage interview at that set.

There are other essay prizes available throughout the year. Look out for posters around your law school and check the legal press and Inns' and chambers' websites for details of competitions.

*Vacation Schemes*

Vacation schemes or "vac schemes" are the solicitors' equivalent of mini-pupillages. Usually lasting between two weeks and a month, they are excellent experience and are often funded (the big City firms pay around £250 per week). Vacation schemes fill up quickly and can be extremely competitive. Apply early to increase your chances of getting a place.

With varying levels of structure, vacation schemes can include work-shops, lectures and assessed problems as well as hands-on experience of solicitors' work. Having one or more vacation schemes on your application form shows chambers that you have sensibly considered the alternative legal career. It also shows that you know what solicitors look for when instructing counsel. Importantly, having experienced both, you will be able to satisfy yourself that the Bar is your preferred career.

*Former Vacation Scheme Student*
I undertook a vac scheme at a 'Magic Circle' firm while still at law school. It gave me a real insight into the solicitors' profession. It's very different from life at the Bar. This meant that I was able to answer the

inevitable pupillage interview question 'why do you want to be a barrister?' with the conviction arising from actual experience of the alternative.

When applying for a vacation scheme, think carefully about the area in which you wish to practise. Vacation schemes enable you to work in a field which you may not otherwise experience through your legal studies. Research firms carefully. If you want to focus your experiences, target either specialist firms or large firms with specialist departments in the areas of law in which you are interested.

*Former Vacation Scheme Student*
I was sure I wanted to be a barrister. I'd enjoyed my minis and done well at mooting. I thought I would do a vac scheme for pupillage interview conversation but to my surprise I loved it! There is a real buzz and a great sense of teamwork that I hadn't anticipated. I was offered a training contract and haven't looked back.

*Specialist Work Experience*

If you have identified an area of law that you wish to practise, you can use work experience to show chambers that your interest is genuine. Think about all the elements of your potential practice and draw up a list of places where you could work which would give you some insight not just into the area of law, but also the people who will be affected by it. So, for example, if you are interested in clinical negligence, start by visiting the General Medical Council (GMC) or doing a vacation scheme at a specialist firm. You could then spend time working in a hospital, volunteer as a hospital visitor or visit Hospital Radio to get an understanding of patients' concerns and priorities. Perhaps you could visit a Coroner's Inquest or even watch an autopsy to see if you can cope with the blood and gore. Such activities do not necessarily involve a major time commitment: some can take as little as an afternoon. When it comes to filling out your applications, however, these experiences will show your interest in chambers' practice is both real and informed.

Further suggestions for specialist work experience are provided in Chapter 20 which tackles each practice area in detail.

*Marshalling*

This is where you sit "on the bench" next to a judge during a case. It can last any length of time from a morning to a couple of weeks. You will almost certainly be given the opportunity to discuss the case with the judge. Through such experience, you may witness a number of different styles of advocacy, all from the judge's perspective. This can be invaluable when honing your own technique.

*A Law Student*

I spent a day marshalling. The barristers were not at all impressive—very unprepared and barely audible. This actually made for an excellent learning experience. It is often easier to see what someone is doing wrong and I am now careful not to repeat their mistakes. It is much harder to put your finger on exactly what a good advocate is doing right when they make it look so natural and easy.

Marshalling can be organised through your Inn.

## Long-Term Legal Activities and Experience

Long-term work experience can be ideal if, like most applicants, you fail to get pupillage first time round. The ideas below include some suggestions, a few of which can only be embarked upon following the BPTC. These are an excellent way to spend time gaining experience while also getting paid.

*Postgraduate Study*

With the competition for pupillage intensifying and chambers moving towards their own specialisms, one popular way to improve your CV before applying is to undertake some further study. The most common option is to take an LLM (or the BCL) in the area of law in which you want to specialise.

A Master of Laws, "LLM", is a one-year course which takes you beyond a regular law degree. The LLM allows you to study an area of law to an advanced level which can be excellent experience if you wish to apply to a specialist set in the field in which you have studied. It is offered at universities throughout England and Wales and you will need a good degree to apply.

A Bachelor of Civil Laws, "BCL", is Oxford University's equivalent to the LLM and is said to be the most prestigious course of its kind in England and Wales. It is full-time and only on offer to those with a first-class degree.

## Judicial Assistants in the Court of Appeal and the Supreme Court

One of the most exciting forms of legal experience available is to work as a Judicial Assistant. Judicial Assistants assist the Law Lords and Lords Justices of Appeal through such work as clarifying issues prior to cases, structuring the case where the documents and submissions are not already well-presented, and undertaking research.

There are ten judicial assistant positions at any one time and you can serve a period of three to twelve months. Previously, judicial assistants had to have completed pupillage but these rules have now been relaxed and pre-pupillage applicants can apply for a post. Positions are advertised three times annually in *The Times* and on HM Court Service website. See *www.hmcourts-service.gov.uk/cms/7629.htm* for more details.

## Legal Practice Clerking

After you have completed your BPTC, you can work as a legal practice clerk. Legal practice clerks represent clients throughout the country in cases which do not require advocates with higher rights of audience (barristers gain these only after completing six months of pupillage). These cases include mortgage repossessions, bankruptcy, summary judgment applications and small claims trials.

There are three different levels of case which these clerks can do, with three corresponding levels of training (ranging from seminars and workshops to mock trials). Legal practice clerking not only allows you to start cutting your teeth before getting into chambers, it is also paid. See *www.lpc-law.co.uk* for further details.

## Paralegalling

Paralegals are paid, legally-trained assistants to solicitors, and work in solicitors' firms or other organisations such as the CAB or trade unions. While there are official qualifications enabling you to work as a paralegal, most firms do not require them. The work entails much of the behind-the-scenes preparation that goes into a case. The lawyer whom you are assisting should check all the work that you carry out (the ultimate responsibility for it lies with them) so it provides an excellent opportunity to learn.

You should expect to be doing at least some fairly dull, administrative tasks. However, the amount of this kind of work can vary enormously from firm to firm depending on its size and which department you are working in. For example, some firms have dedicated bundling and photocopying departments, whereas in others this job may fall to you. It is therefore worth trying to find out as much as possible in advance about your responsibilities. In the corporate department of a Magic Circle firm you may spend your days proofreading contracts or "bibling" (indexing bundles of documents). In others you may have more responsibility: attending client meetings and taking proofs of evidence; attending hearings; researching points of law; drafting documents; and even assuming overall responsibility for smaller cases. Some firms may take you on to assist with one large case or you may be assisting more generally in a particular department or across departments. The bottom line is that paralegal jobs are extremely varied.

Some people find that there is a link between whether a firm has trainees and the quality of your role as a paralegal. If there are trainees it may be that the paralegal role is not as interesting. It depends on the individual firm so do your research before you apply.

> **Tip:** If you are called for an interview for a paralegal role, be prepared to demonstrate an awareness that you may be required to carry out everyday administration and that you are not too grand for the job.

If you are interested in becoming a paralegal, check solicitors' websites for advertisements and apply directly, or sign up with a legal recruitment agency. Paralegal roles are often for rolling three month or six month contracts. If there are no paralegal positions available, you may be able to work as a legal secretary or a legal temp doing similar work until a position arises.

*Outdoor Clerking*

Outdoor clerks are paid to assist solicitors with work outside the solicitors' office (hence the title). This can involve a range of work including assisting Counsel at court, filing documents with the court and taking notes in conferences or during a case.

Contact solicitors' firms directly for outdoor clerking positions.

*Court Ushering*

Court ushers ensure the smooth running of the court. This includes preparing the courtroom, labelling the evidence and checking that all the relevant parties (lawyers, jury and witnesses) are present at the right time. In a similar way to marshalling, this work will give you an insider's view into the workings of a courtroom and the opportunity to watch many different styles of advocacy, while being paid.

See *www.hmcourts-service.gov.uk* and *www.skillsforjustice.com*.

*Death Row Work*

A rising trend among law students is to work for charities such as Amicus and Reprieve to get prisoners abroad off Death Row. Volunteer placements normally last between three and six months and take place overseas. This work may involve the more mundane elements of case preparation such as administrative assistance and legal research but can also be more exciting. You could find yourself interviewing witnesses, assisting lawyers and carrying out investigative work unparalleled in England and Wales. In the USA this can include such things as approaching jurors to ensure that the trial process was legal—a practice which does not exist here.

There are also opportunities to volunteer in the charities' London offices. See *www.amicus-alj.org* and *www.reprieve.org.uk*.

*The Legal Press*

Get involved with the legal press. It's a good opportunity to show future chambers that you have the potential to adopt an analytical and evaluative approach that is prized by barristers. It will show that you can actually write about and argue about the law in a coherent way. Plus, it's an excellent way of making contacts with people who might be helpful later on.

*Nicholas McBride*

There is a tremendous amount of written material generated about the law every week. There are therefore various opportunities to work in the legal press, whether at a legal publisher, newspaper, magazine or student publication. This should improve your writing skills but will also keep you up to date about changes and developments in the law.

Alternatively, you could apply to work at one of the legal search engines or online databases.

Look on their websites for any available opportunities.

If you are unable to find work in this field, why not start writing a legal blog—known as a "blawg"? Your name may become known in the legal community and, if you write well and are lucky, it may lead to a job opportunity. Very importantly, change all names and identifying details where appropriate.

# 16 FURTHER NON-LEGAL EXPERIENCE

> When you're deciding what to do, do something you're interested in. Lots of applicants will have similar things on their CVs. You must be able to talk convincingly about what you've done and express what you've enjoyed or learned from the experience. Someone who has, for example, worked as a community nurse or raised a family and who can explain why this was important to them and how it has led to their personal development may be regarded as more impressive than someone who has done a chain of short term placements at NGOs but can't articulate the reason for doing them or the skills they learnt in the process.
>
> *Tessa Hetherington, Matrix Chambers*

## Employment

Any non-legal paid employment can be a valuable asset to your CV and may assist a pupillage application. Through such work you can demonstrate other skills which may be useful in practice. These could be anything from an understanding of commercial markets if you have worked in, say, banking, to creativity and teamwork if you have worked as a chef.

## Voluntary Work

A career as a barrister will expose you to people from a variety of backgrounds, often at difficult times in their lives. One of the hardest challenges barristers can face is finding the balance between empathy and professionalism. Beyond being intrinsically rewarding, voluntary work can teach you this balance.

There is a huge range of charity work available so you should easily find a field that appeals to you. You could work for a housing charity such as Shelter or St Mungo's if your interest lies in landlord and tenant, Greenpeace if environmental law appeals or Amnesty if you wish to specialise in human rights law (see Chapter 20 for more ideas).

**Hobbies and Interests**

Non-law hobbies and interests are absolutely essential. They are one of the few ways you can inject a little colour into your pupillage applications and, with so much time invested in law-related activities, they may also keep you sane. The rewards of taking a little time for yourself and developing your own interests are plentiful. You will make new friends, learn new skills and increase your confidence.

> Your mind is like a muscle: it gets bigger with exercise. The more you exercise your mind the better your capacity for thinking. But like any other muscle it needs recovery time—it can't be exercising all the time otherwise it will blow up. You need to take time off, to do things other than law. An essential part of learning the law is to take a break from the law.
>
> *Nicholas McBride*

Dedicate some time to pursuing an interest. It could be anything from playing a musical instrument to acting or joining a sports team. Just be sure it is something you enjoy. For almost all extra-curricular pastimes, you will find that there are transferable skills which you can mention at interview.

Whatever your interests, try developing them in a way that will make your CV stand out. For example, if you enjoy jogging, could you run a marathon? If you enjoy creative writing, could you organise a story-writing competition at a local primary school or library? If you like listening to music, could you review local concerts for an online magazine?

See Chapter 21 on Applications for more ideas.

# SECTION 5: CHOOSING YOUR PRACTICE

# 17 THE EMPLOYED BAR

Most barristers are self-employed, working independently within chambers. For about 3,000 barristers in England and Wales, however, the structure of practice is very different. These barristers work at the Employed Bar. They work for large organisations under a similar employment structure to most solicitors. The Employed Bar offers the job security that stems from being an employee, as well as benefits such as a pension, health insurance and maternity or paternity leave. It can also provide unique exposure to certain types of work. Before you sign up for the Independent Bar, consider the advantages of employed practice.

There are career opportunities for barristers to work in:

- the Government Legal Service (GLS);
- the Crown Prosecution Service (CPS);
- the Armed Forces;
- the European Commission;
- large firms of solicitors with in-house counsel; and
- some large non-legal corporations.

Some of these institutions also offer their own pupillages although there are very few places and competition can be intense. Further information is available from the institutions' websites.

## Experience of Pupillage with the GLS

My pupillage was with the Treasury Solicitor's Department (TSol), which is a member of the GLS. I spent eight months at TSol and at what was then the Department for Education and Skills. The remaining four months were spent on secondment to a set of chambers specialising in public and commercial law.

The range of work was invigorating: from immigration, education and employment matters to problems involving European Community and human rights law. I experienced a variety of different tribunals at both first instance and appellate level, right up to the House of Lords and I was also involved in steering some new legislation through Parliament. In short, my pupillage gave me a flavour of the litigious, advisory and legislative business that characterises administrative and public law practice.

The high profile, and often controversial, nature of government means that in the GLS you are never far from involvement in interesting matters of law, fact or political and media debate. Since qualifying, I have continued to be involved with high profile, high value and legally interesting work having acted for clients participating in judicial review proceedings, group litigation, ADR, inquests and a public inquiry.

Being an employed barrister takes you across the boundary between barrister and solicitor. In these respects, it's more like the fused profession that exists in other common law jurisdictions such as Canada, New Zealand, or the USA. Day to day, I liaise with witnesses, experts and counsel, draft statements of case and other legal documents and advise and represent my client as one might expect. But the role of a government lawyer isn't limited to advising on legal problems and disputes facing public bodies and their constituent interests, we also assist in developing and implementing government policy whether through the introduction of enabling legislation or otherwise. The job demands more than just legal acumen and the orthodox skills of an advocate or a legislative draftsman. You have to be a manager, an investigator, often a diplomat, and of course you are a civil servant too.

If you are interested in working for the GLS, be sure to have a commitment to public service, an interest in the nature of government business, and an enthusiasm to develop the range of your expertise as a lawyer and as an advocate in Whitehall, Westminster, and beyond.

I don't think it is any coincidence that opportunities within the GLS are highly sought after. Being at the heart of government is natural territory for any lawyer.

*Simon Ramsden, TSol*

**Alternatives for the Second Six Months of Pupillage:** There are several alternatives to traditional pupillage which fulfil the Bar Council's training requirements for your second six. Some last for the entire six months whereas others will be for a much shorter period. Options include:

- A six month "stage" in a legal department of the European Commission in Brussels, Luxembourg or London.

- Six months working with a lawyer in another EU member state.

- A month spent with a pro bono service such as FRU or a law centre.

- A month spent with a solicitor or professional who does work similar to that of a pupil supervisor.

This list is not exhaustive. Approval must be sought from the Bar Standards Board Qualifications Committee prior to commencement.

# 18 THE PROVINCIAL BAR

One important choice to be made is where you want to practise. England and Wales are divided up into "circuits". These are the Midland, North Eastern, Northern, South Eastern, Wales and Chester, and Western Circuits.

Some people are quick to dismiss practice outside London; they forget that the provincial Bar has much to offer. While the information contained within this book relates to the whole Bar, both London and the circuits, listed below are some of the advantages of a practice outside the capital.

**Quality of Experience and Chances of Tenancy**

It is generally agreed that provincial sets, unlike their London counterparts, will only offer as many pupillages as they have space for tenants. Statistically, therefore, your chances of being taken on in a provincial set are far higher. The knock-on effect is that during your pupillage you will not feel in constant competition with other pupils. You will therefore be able to relax and concentrate on doing your best.

The quality of pupillage tends to be far higher at provincial sets. It's true that there are generally fewer pupils per set so your chances of getting taken on are higher. But people forget to look at what this means from chambers' point of view. It means that all pupils are seen as future members of chambers. As a result, chambers invest far more time and effort in their pupils' development.

*Giles Cannock, Kings Chambers, Manchester*

**Quality and Breadth of Work**

Because there are fewer barristers in the provinces, you will generally be given better quality work earlier than you would in London. Moreover, with the exception of some very specialist areas such as IP or competition, it is not true that you must be based in the capital to work on the most exciting cases.

In addition, you will have more time to choose your specialism; chambers' practice areas at the junior end tend to be much broader.

Having a broad base of experience is a great benefit regardless of the area in which you want to specialise later. You learn the absolute basics and that's crucial. I am often surprised when I see barristers in court who did not have the breadth of practice in their early years: they struggle compared with barristers who did have such breadth.

*Lee Reynolds, Apex Chambers, Cardiff*

## Lifestyle

London is expensive. The cost of living is often significantly higher than it is in the provinces. However, it is not necessarily the case that you get paid proportionately more in London to counterbalance this. This begins from pupillage as chambers with branches in London and the provinces will often have the same pupillage awards throughout, regardless of location. The result is that quality of life tends to be higher if you practise outside London. Provincial cities tend to have easily accessible countryside and leisure time facilities. In addition, your journey to and from work can take a fraction of the time and be considerably more pleasant.

I have a much higher standard of living compared with those of my seniority who work in London.

*Leila Benyounes, Park Lane Plowden, Leeds*

## Size of the Bar

At the provincial Bar it is not at all unusual to know all the barristers who practise your area of law. Add to this the circuit dinners, where everyone from judge to pupil is invited, and you can see why the provincial Bar is known for its camaraderie.

There are a great many myths about the provincial Bar. People don't realise that it's worth sparing a thought for the provinces. They often think and assume that the only good chambers are in London and the provincial Bar is second rate but this simply is not the case. The provinces offer an equal quality of work and more of it, coupled with a better quality of life. Don't assume that London is the only place to be. It's not.

*Richard Tetlow, Exchange Chambers, Manchester*

# 19 SPECIALISATION AND THE BAR

## The Trend Towards Specialisation

Though lots of people think that being a barrister necessarily involves frequent days in court with dramatic cross-examinations and passionate speeches, the reality of life at the Bar, for some, is very different.

> You need to consider which area you want to practise. There's not just one Bar: there are many Bars. There's a Commercial Bar, a Tax Bar, an Intellectual Property Bar, a Criminal Bar, a Family Bar, an Employment Bar. All of these are individual specialisms and they are very different from each other.
>
> *Lord Grabiner QC, One Essex Court*

> A barrister specialising in, say, competition law has very little in common with one practising criminal law. In many ways, they are completely different jobs.
>
> *Maya Lester, Brick Court Chambers*

Your choice of specialism will define how much of your time you spend in court, what type of clients you have, where you work and how much you earn.

There was a time when almost all barristers began their careers in the Magistrates' and County Courts with a mixed common law practice. If you ask these now-senior barristers, most will tell you that the skills they learnt there—how to detect the mood of the judge, cross-examine witnesses and handle difficult clients—are all skills on which they continue to rely in their current practice.

> I once read that the life of the barrister, particularly the young barrister, is a 'series of alarms and excursions', called on to attend court here and there, often at very short notice and sometimes a very long way away. I

discovered very much what this meant when I was required to be in Goole one day and then Truro the next. I sent my clerks a postcard from Goole, to show my appreciation. It is during these early days in practice that you should be prepared to take on as wide a range of work as possible and show yourself willing and able to work tirelessly and effectively.

*Colin Wynter QC, Devereux Chambers*

The training of junior barristers is now somewhat different. Nowadays, most London and some provincial sets target their expertise towards specialist areas of law. This can have the effect of restricting the practice of all members of chambers to those specialist areas, and may reduce advocacy experience at the junior end to a bare minimum. Accordingly, pupils and juniors have fewer opportunities to develop their skills by practising a broad range of law.

There are two reasons for this change. First, solicitor-advocates are now able to appear in all courts. As a result, solicitors are increasingly reluctant to outsource work to counsel which they can do themselves. This has introduced more competition, particularly at the junior end of the Bar. Secondly, as solicitors have themselves specialised, they have demanded that the Bar specialise too, and the Bar has been nervous about insisting that advocacy and judgment on your feet is a specialism. Consequently, barristers have focused on narrower and narrower areas.

Even at the very early stage of filling out your first application form, you may be dictating the fields in which you will practise for the rest of your life. It is therefore important to keep this in mind from the outset.

### Factors Informing your Choice of Specialism

*Playing to your Strengths*

You should be realistic about where your strengths lie and where your skills and experience will best support you.

Imagine, for example, you have spent the last three summers mentoring underprivileged children with Anti-Social Behaviour Orders and working in your local CAB but your degree result was not as strong as it could have been. In this case, a criminal or family set may value your ability to build relationships with young people who have become cynical of authority and your experience with a range of issues relating to poverty, housing and mental health. At a commercial chambers, however, your lack of proven academic brilliance may mean you wouldn't even make the first round interview list.

Do what interests you, but be realistic about where your experiences can take you.

*Remuneration*

Some barristers find a flawless cross-examination or a winning closing speech reward enough. For others, money is everything. Most barristers are somewhere between these extremes. Whether or not money is a major motivating factor, it is important to have some idea of likely earnings before making your choice. Income at the Bar can vary significantly and it is difficult to predict with any certainty. Even within the same practice area, different barristers of the same seniority can earn surprisingly different amounts. Nevertheless, at least for the early years of practice, there is one basic rule that holds true: you will earn more if you practise civil than if you practise public or criminal law. Public and criminal barristers will typically be paid by the Government (either through the Legal Services Commission or another public body) whose budget constraints restrict the amount they pay to lawyers.

*The Future*

Whilst the demand for barristers practising in some areas will stay fairly constant, others are more subject to the fluctuations of the economy and changes in politics. Commercial lawyers, for example, can find that the nature of their practice varies dramatically depending on whether the economy is booming or in recession. If you have in mind a very narrow area of commercial practice, you might be wise to acquire an under-standing of the global economy and how changes to that economy will affect your career. Considering such factors as economics, politics and the current zeitgeist can help you to predict the legal "growth areas" of the future. Thirty years ago, European law, immigration and human rights were not fashionable areas. Today these fields make front-page news and the lawyers that specialised in them early are benefiting accordingly.

Another consideration is the potential for policy change in public funding. The Criminal Bar in particular is currently facing great uncertainty.

Funding has repeatedly been cut and more seismic changes seem likely (see, for example, the Carter Review). The same uncertainty applies—albeit to a lesser extent—to all publicly-funded work. Of course, the existence of risk and uncertainty should not mean that you do not apply. If you are determined, committed and confident then do not let these risks put you off. Just be sure that your decision is an informed one.

At a certain point you are absolutely bound to ask why you are doing what you are doing. The enormous excitement of slipping off the pink (or white) tape and seeing your name on the backsheet—printed if you are lucky—eventually fades and every day becomes like the one before. Burn out is a problem at the Bar because hours are long, frequently anti-social and always unpredictable. Every barrister's significant other knows what it feels like to be stood up on ten minutes' notice and to try and tell the story of their day to someone whose eyes are involuntarily closing.

If you enjoy the long-game where strategic and tactical goals are the main item then think commercial or criminal fraud work. If standing up for the underdog is what does it for you then consider public law or standard crime. If separating warring parties with the minimum of aggro is key then think about family or partnership work. But do at least try to consider how you will feel on a wet Wednesday in February 10 years hence.

*Simon Myerson QC, St Paul's Chambers, Leeds and*
*Byrom Street Chambers, Manchester*

*The Future of Litigation: Mediation?*

Mediation, a form of Alternative Dispute Resolution (ADR), relies on a neutral third party to help resolve conflict by encouraging non-adversarial communication and fluid remedies.

Mediation gives barristers the opportunity to practise a different style of advocacy from that of the courtroom and to exercise a level of creativity that traditional litigation rarely allows. Although "sometimes traditional litigation suits the parties' needs best, the cost, both financially and emotionally, tends to be huge" says Karl Mackie of the Centre for Effective Dispute Resolution (CEDR). According to Mackie, "in litigation, clients often expect a war—they want you to put forward the best points and fight. Mediation is not really about that. It is about weighing and even sometimes blurring the issues in order to reach compromise settlements to find areas of consensus and mutuality."

Mackie says that the days of "real-men-don't-eat-quiche-scepticism" about mediation are long gone: "both in terms of philosophy and professional recognition, the Bar has swung completely behind it". Barristers are typically involved in mediation in one of two ways, either as an advocate for one of the parties, or (when more senior) as the mediator. In both roles, success demands "creativity, active listening and an ability to relate to different personalities" says Mackie. Developing these skills has obvious benefits to the practice of litigation. But be warned: many who train in mediation struggle to return to litigation: "it is often difficult to run practices side by side unless you're mentally quite flexible" says Mackie.

In certain areas (for example, commercial, family and construction), the Bar is increasingly turning to mediation as a faster, cheaper and often more effective way to resolve clients' problems. Whether mediation appeals or you are set on courtroom advocacy, ensure that you research your practice area and chambers thoroughly and understand what your future practice may entail. Mediation is here to stay.

## A Catch-22 Situation

While many students recognise that the Bar is becoming specialised, they are uncomfortable committing to one narrow area of law so early in their careers. Their experience of practice areas may initially be limited to academic study. Naturally, they want a more realistic understanding before committing to one area—otherwise how can they make an informed choice? But by choosing their chambers they immediately narrow their options and, before they know it, their career may be pigeon-holed into one particular specialism.

How should you approach applications if this is the case?

### Experience a Range of Work

Make a concerted effort to experience as many areas of practice as possible through mini-pupillages. You could approach your Inn to see if there is someone to whom you can speak about their practice. Read around any area you are considering. Doing these things may not give you the confidence to choose an area, but may help you to dismiss certain areas.

## Join a Set with Many Specialisms

There are still some chambers that have not restricted their practice areas and continue to practise general common law. In such chambers you will be able to have a very mixed practice for the first few years and then decide where you want to specialise. The advantages to this are clear: you have the time to assess where your strengths lie and what work you enjoy. For these sets, the true specialism is advocacy.

Don't get hung up about knowing at Bar school what you want to do. In the first 12 months of practice it is a great advantage to try to experience as many different areas as possible. You need to focus on where you want to be in 10 years' time.

*Giles Cannock, Kings Chambers, Manchester*

While there are some excellent chambers in London where such a range of work is still possible, you may find that practising in the provinces in an advantage in this respect. With fewer sets, there is usually a wider range of work within each.

In my year of pupillage I found that it's good to take any work you're given. Have a look at everything. You can work out which area you're best at later. For the first few years, the more that goes into the mix, the better you become as an advocate.

*Richard Tetlow, Exchange Chambers*

# 20 PRACTICE AREAS

## Chancery

Chancery is an extremely diverse area of practice. It comprises two branches. "Traditional Chancery" includes the areas of probate, property, pensions and trusts. "Commercial Chancery" includes the areas of company, partnership, fraud and insolvency. The underlying legal threads common to all areas are the principles of equity (one of the seven core areas of law).

Because of the documentary nature of the work, for most cases there will be a vast amount of reading to be done before you can even start looking at legal principles. An essential skill therefore, according to Ruth Holtham of Serle Court, is "the ability to analyse a great deal of information very fast whilst retaining the details". You also need "independence and stamina to keep going through the long hours—especially when you are in court".

Be prepared to spend a lot of time reading in your room. It is hard work: "it can be really difficult to mug up an area of law as fast as you need to: you sometimes have to get up to speed overnight in areas you've never addressed before". What's more, with such a broad range of underlying subjects, it may be easy to feel as if you never make any progress.

Those hours spent in your room are generously rewarded: chancery pays well and there is no shortage of work. Although some areas are affected by downturns in global markets, as a chancery practitioner your breadth of practice provides a level of protection. As one area dries up, another explodes as companies adapt their strategies to encompass new regulations and realities.

*Pros:*

- Great variety of work and lots of it, regardless of the economic climate.

- Extremely well paid.

- Intellectually stimulating.

- Ability to shape your practice so that you can keep relatively predictable hours by, for example, doing exclusively paperwork.

*Cons:*

- Very little oral advocacy.

- Lots of factually complex paperwork and difficult law.

*Ideas for Work Experience:*

- An internship in an investment bank or in the City.

- Any work which gives you exposure to the world of commerce and teaches you what business clients want.

## Clinical Negligence

Just like other professionals, health practitioners sometimes make mistakes. These mistakes can cause injuries ranging from the very minor to the catastrophic. Clinical negligence addresses the legal consequences of such mistakes. Most commonly this will be through claims for compensation against the doctor, dentist or other clinician involved. At other times, clinical negligence practitioners will attend Coroners' Inquests, disciplinary hearings at the General Medical Council (GMC) or Inquiries (Shipman, Bristol Hearts etc). Finally, there are an ever-increasing number of applications arising out of ethical issues where parties seek declarations as to the legality of providing or withdrawing life-saving treatment.

"The issues you are addressing are fascinating—on medical grounds, ethical grounds and as an advocate" says Michael Mylonas of 3 Serjeants' Inn. You will be dealing with highly sensitive issues and fighting for results that really make a difference to your clients, not just in terms of money, but to their future wellbeing. Feelings are strong on both sides. The claimants will often feel violated by a botched procedure that has permanently impaired their ability to enjoy life. The doctors may feel angry and let down because someone is fundamentally questioning their hard-won professional ability and reputation, thereby jeopardising their practice and livelihood. In ethical cases the stakes are higher still. Questions of life or death are being decided and it is the advocate's job to ensure that the court has the best possible evidence before it on which to assess whether life-saving treatment should be withdrawn or continued. A good knowledge of the law combined with an understanding of the medical issues is critical. So too is the ability to ask the right questions of the experts so all the relevant evidence is obtained. There's little point thinking of a new and clever argument in favour of continuing treatment two months after the patient concerned has been taken off a ventilator and has died.

Your role will be to empathise while giving sometimes unwelcome advice about the merits and likely outcome. This advice regularly involves complex questions of law and fact which are often causation-based. However difficult, you must learn to separate your emotions about the case from your legal advice. "Although it can be difficult," says Judith Rogerson of 1 Crown Office Row Chambers, "it is important to remain emotionally detached—especially when you get to know the clients so well. Your advice must be impartial and level-headed."

"There is also a managerial side to the work" says Michael Mylonas, "often it's not really about law, it's about strategy: getting all the evidence in place to show the other side that they are going to lose and persuading them to give up at an early stage."

Trials are inherently unpredictable in every area of the law, but this is especially true of clinical negligence. It is very common to have two or more expert witnesses presenting the court with directly conflicting opinions. "For this reason," says Rogerson "most cases settle because the risks of going to trial are just too great for both parties". This will impact upon your practice: most of your advocacy will be done during applications, at the GMC or through negotiations.

*Pros:*

- Interesting ethical and legal issues.

- Winning a case means a lot to a client—whether claimant or defendant.

- Variety of work.

- Variety of tribunal—Crown Court, GMC, High Court.

*Cons:*

- Can be quite technical, emotionally draining and even gory.

- Lots of paperwork with few cases actually making it to trial.

*Ideas for Work Experience:*

- Any clinical experience—whether in a doctor's surgery, an NHS Trust or a Coroner's Office.

- Attend hearings at the GMC.

## Commercial

Commercial litigation involves disputes about contracts. Issues can relate to banking, insurance and reinsurance, shipping and general contractual matters.

Clients range from private individual shareholders to multinational banks or insurance companies. Because of the English courts' worldwide reputation for excellence, it is quite common for there to be an international element to the work. The build-up to trial can take several years, with important applications made throughout. For this reason, your practice will be dominated by a few very large files—quite unlike many other areas where you have new cases coming in every day. As a result, commercial law attracts some of the most cerebral students—"you are surrounded by really clever people" says James Duffy of Fountain Court. "If you let your standards slip, you can be sure someone will trip you up" agrees Richard Mott of One Essex Court, "if you're even slightly competitive, you get a real feeling of adrenaline."

Arbitration, negotiation and other Alternative Dispute Resolution (ADR) mechanisms also play a major role in commercial practice. In fact very few cases end up in court because the majority settle. It is therefore crucial that the commercial barrister is an excellent strategist, identifying the client's needs and building the case accordingly. Demonstrating an understanding of the market is essential to succeed here. Pupils must be able to identify what a business wants and know how to achieve its goals.

In your first few years, depending on your set, you can usually expect to be involved in a broad range of cases. You will be given a few small cases of your own—perhaps County Court trials—but most of your time will be spent acting as second Junior on large cases. Whatever you find yourself doing, "academic excellence is probably the first thing that is looked for" says Duffy. There is considerable legal research so expect many hours in the library reading cases and textbooks. "I am usually in court once or twice a week and the rest of the time I'm doing paperwork."

Your instructing solicitors will often be large City law firms or the legal departments of major banks who are, according to Mott, "absolutely top-notch and very stimulating to work with". Such firms have high demands. If they need something done, they will expect it done quickly and accurately. Thus, hours can be long and unpredictable; but earnings for the successful commercial barrister are substantial.

*Pros:*

- Interesting and intellectually stimulating legal issues.

- High-profile litigation often puts you at the cutting edge of commerce.

- Choosing the right strategy in the early stages of litigation can define the end result, which can be very satisfying.

- Well paid.

*Cons:*

- Lots of work getting to grips with complex, often dry, documents or doing legal research with limited oral advocacy.

- Long and sometimes unpredictable hours.

*Ideas for Work Experience:*

- Work in an investment bank or another financial institution.

- Run a small business.

## Competition

"Competition law is the intersection between commercial and public law," says Naina Patel of Blackstone Chambers. Designed to ensure that the markets work to the ultimate benefit of consumers, competition law prevents companies entering into price-fixing cartels or abusing monopoly positions.

Competition is a combination of public and private law—domestic as well as European—with substantive economic analysis also playing a large part. "At the moment I'm doing a case that involves the interaction of human rights law and competition law. Although specialised, competition relates to other areas of law as well," says Maya Lester of Brick Court

Chambers. As Julian Gregory of Monkton Chambers observes, cases cover a broad range of facts as well as law: "I was recently arguing about how much space a sports logo may take up on the players' clothing at international tennis Grand Slams".

With a practice in this area, don't expect to be in court every day—or even every month. On those occasions when you do get to court, it will often be on very large, high-profile cases where you will be a Junior or even a second Junior. In this respect, Lester accepts that "it's probably not the best way to become an advocate". "However," she continues, "if you like the interaction of legal and economic principles then it's fascinating: it gets you deeply under the skin of companies and allows you to see how they work". You will often be working alongside those in very senior positions of major companies for whom competition issues are a serious concern.

Competition law will appeal to a certain type of person. A proven record of outstanding academic performance is a prerequisite. "Unlike other areas of law," says Gregory, "there's not much of a mismatch between the academic study of this area and the practice of it at the Bar." This means you should be able to assess whether or not it is for you before you apply.

One thing to note when considering this area is that very few sets do primarily competition work. Most chambers combine it with other areas—typically European and commercial law. Even if you go to a specialist set, you may find you begin with more general commercial work and specialise only after pupillage.

*Pros:*

- Intellectually stimulating.

- Potential for high-profile cases in a fast-developing area of law.

- Well paid.

- The small Bar gives a sense of camaraderie.

*Cons:*

- There can be little oral advocacy—though a few people do find themselves in court relatively regularly on matters such as applying for injunctions.

- Lots of technical economic data to analyse.

*Ideas for Work Experience:*

- Work experience in the Office of Fair Trading.
- Work in the competition department of a firm of solicitors.
- A course which gives you an understanding of basic economic principles.

## Construction

Construction practice involves disputes concerning the work of construction professionals such as architects, engineers or building contractors. As a subset of commercial law, an interest—and proven strength—in contract law is essential.

In the early years of practice, most of your work will be for a senior barrister rather than being instructed by a solicitor in your own capacity. There is a mundane element—"you spend a lot of time just assimilating the facts" says Lucie Briggs of Atkin Chambers, who was recently working on a case which involved over 300 lever arch files of information. Expect to spend around 80 per cent of your time on paperwork. You have to be "very interested in the detail" according to Jennie Gillies of 4 Pump Court. Indeed, she continues, "quite a lot of construction practice involves working in big teams, and, as a Junior, you will be doing a lot of paperwork and disclosure. At this level, it's more akin to a junior solicitor's work." When not working for a Senior, you can expect to be in court in your own right "once every few weeks" says Briggs.

Disputes will usually end in one of three places. The smallest cases (those you will handle as a Junior) will be heard in the County Court. Larger cases go to the specialist Technology and Construction Court. Many cases do not reach court at all, ending with Alternative Dispute Resolution (ADR) such as Mediation, Arbitration or Adjudication. Because of the large amounts of money at stake, the complexity of the issues and the frequent need to preserve an ongoing relationship, parties can be eager to avoid a courtroom battle. As a result, ADR is becoming an increasingly popular way to resolve construction disputes. An understanding of the principles of ADR is essential for any would-be construction specialist.

To succeed in construction you will need intellect, analysis and the ability to assimilate detailed and complicated facts. "A curious and enquiring nature is also an advantage—for one recent case I had to learn the detail of how an oil rig works" says Briggs. Developing a rapport with the client is essential. Client contacts can be anyone from building-site professionals to the directors of large multinational corporations, says Gillies. No matter what factual and legal challenges you face, they must all be reduced to concise submissions. There are no grandiose jury speeches here; what is required, according to Briggs, is "good technical advocacy".

If this is your area you must be "very hard-working and robust" warns Gillies. The financial rewards are there for those who succeed.

*Pros:*

- Intellectually challenging.

- Lots of well paid work.

- Insight into interesting industries.

- Interesting range of clients.

*Cons:*

- Large amounts of paperwork and not many advocacy opportunities for the first few years.

- Long hours spent assimilating facts and understanding the case.

*Ideas for Work Experience:*

- Work for one of the larger construction companies, architects, building or civil engineers.

- Go to the Technology and Construction Court and watch the style of advocacy.

## Crime

For many, the Criminal Bar is a calling. If you want courtroom drama, the excitement of oral advocacy, and the pressure of knowing that your poor performance may cost your clients their liberty, crime may be the area for you.

From the very first day of your second six months of pupillage, you will probably be on your feet prosecuting or defending very minor offences, or at bail hearings and pleas in mitigation. You can expect to be in court almost every day for your first few years of practice, starting in the Magistrates' Courts on minor motoring offences and moving up to the Crown Court for more serious offences like common assault. A major advantage of the Criminal Bar is that there is different work for every level of seniority. As your experience grows, so does the severity of the offence that you will defend or prosecute. There are also opportunities to work with a senior barrister on complex cases.

Confidence, drive and the ability to stand up and present a case even after little preparation are the essentials. In the early years, according to Kevin Toomey of 2 Bedford Row, "client and solicitor care are probably the most important part of your practice: the complex law comes later". After your first few years, "tenacity, a good sense of humour and an insight into the reasoning of a jury" are crucial to long-term success, says Philip Evans of QEB Hollis Whiteman.

Hours are long and much of your time will be spent travelling to distant courts for clients who will not always appreciate you. In addition, says Toomey, "it's physically demanding—you'll be working till 10 most nights and on the 6.30 train the next morning. At all times, says Adam King of QEB Hollis Whiteman, "you must be able to make really difficult decisions, where none of the options is particularly attractive".

With lots of advocacy from the early days, an exciting lifestyle and an endless supply of stories, the Criminal Bar appears to have it all. But dig a little deeper and you find that it is facing serious challenges. Over several years, the Government has been changing the funding structure of publicly-funded work, which will make up most of your practice. This means, high-level white collar fraud aside, you will now earn less practising crime than you will in almost every other area of the Bar. At the same time, solicitor-advocates increasingly appear in court themselves rather than instructing Counsel, reducing the work available at the junior end. These factors combine to mean a career at the Criminal Bar can be a financial gamble. "You need to develop an excellent relationship with your bank manager: it's a real struggle." says one pupil. Indeed, as barrister Alexander Deane says: "Fees are actually getting *lower* each year as the Dutch Auction between chambers worsens. A regular appearance in the Magistrates' Court could once be guaranteed to average out at £100—now it's more like £60. I can attest from personal experience and the experience of others many people who have been in practice for two or three years will regularly only receive £100 a week. Once you factor in tax and expenses it's genuinely true that you'd actually be better off on benefits."

Added to this is the continued uncertainty about the funding of the Criminal Bar following such developments as the Carter Reforms. The Government's approach to funding goes further than just affecting your bank balance: "lots of criminal practitioners just feel undervalued" says Evans.

For some, however, the Criminal Bar, despite its downsides, will still be a highly rewarding vocation.

*Pros:*

- Lots of advocacy in front of both a judge and a jury.

- A variety of clients means no two cases are ever the same.

- Barristers still wear the wig and gown.

- Performing an important social function.

*Cons:*

- Poorly paid at the junior end and often not given the respect it deserves by the profession.

- Difficult to control your practice: clients in particular can be very unpredictable.

*Ideas for Work Experience:*

- Working for the CPS or police.

- Social or charity work, for example with the Howard League for Penal Reform.

## Employment

Employment law covers all disputes arising from relationships in the workplace. One day you may be defending an employer who has allegedly discriminated against a secretary on the grounds of sexual orientation, the next you may be rushing to court to stop an illegal strike crippling a city's transport system. Just as the issues can vary, so too can the clients—anyone from a disgruntled individual to a major corporation, trade union or public authority.

Kathryn Perera of 11KBW has this advice: "if you've ever thought you want to be a criminal barrister but you also want a combination of intellectually challenging law and good pay, then employment law is for you." The types of work on which employment barristers will be instructed seem to be expanding: changes are "substantially driven by Europe" says Perera and the last five years have seen major growth in the area. An example of this growth is the legislation making it unlawful to discriminate on the grounds of age. Edward Mallett of Littleton Chambers agrees that the constantly changing law "keeps you on your toes". "Moreover," says Mallett, "changes are policy driven—so the balance in employment law varies according to the politics of the government of the day."

Advocacy, of which there will be plenty, will typically take place in the Employment Tribunal, which is less formal than a courtroom. This is designed to encourage self-representation. As a result, your opponents could be anyone from a QC to a litigant in person—and sometimes you won't know until you walk into the room. "It helps to be a bit of an adrenaline junkie," says Perera, and to enjoy adapting your approach to the requirements of the day.

Expect to be busy and to work long hours, often with little advance warning. As Perera says, "Sometimes a hearing comes in at the last minute and you just have to work through the night or all weekend to prepare—that's just the nature of the job. You have to do the best you can for your client in the time available". Cases are heard in the Tribunal nearest to where the parties are based, so there is a lot of travel involved.

To succeed at the Employment Bar, empathy is crucial. Passion can be felt on both sides: an employee may feel bullied or degraded, while an employer may feel offended by the accusations made against them or their company. You must be able to instil confidence in your clients, extract the information you need efficiently, separate feelings from facts and assemble your case in clear legal terms. "If you are the right kind of person," says Mallett, "it is a very enjoyable job: to be running cases early in your career, and to have people trust you with such major issues, is fantastic."

*Pros:*

- Lots of advocacy from the outset.

- Interesting clients often with an emotional investment in their case.

- Variety in both facts and law—no two cases are the same.

- Fast-moving, exciting area of law.

*Cons:*

- Your lifestyle can be unpredictable as cases come in at the last minute and require urgent attention.

- Law is generated quickly and it can be a struggle to stay on top of it.

*Ideas for Work Experience:*

- Anything which gives you a feel for being an employee or gives you management experience such as running a small business.

- Work experience at a trade union or CAB.

- Work as a FRU Employment rep.

## Environmental

Environmental law is a rapidly emerging specialism. It can include such fields as planning, European, tort, contract and property. Both the law and the advocacy are varied—you could be in the High Court arguing about the definition of "waste" one day, then defending a multinational corporation in front of a jury the next. One thing that unites all environmental cases, however, is the tendency to be "fact-heavy, dense, and complex in evidence" says Richard Wald of 39 Essex Street. If you relish this sort of work, then this could be the area for you.

To the aspiring environmental barrister, Wald's advice is to "understand and appreciate those other areas in which you will need to practise in order to get into the area that interests you: there are actually very few barristers who practise only environmental law". Typically, the area that leads most easily into environmental law is planning law.

Although practice is fact-intensive and can involve difficult legal issues, don't expect to spend every day reading in a lonely room. You will be working in a team for many of your cases, sometimes with large numbers of experts. As counsel, you will often be expected to lead a team of experts, solicitors and clients. In fact, says Wald, "success is as much about team-work as it is about the correct legal analysis of the issues. You must have the interpersonal skills to be able to get on with a wide range of people."

Wald's advice to those wanting to take on the challenge is that "there is no substitute for getting some form of relevant experience—anything that helps you gain an understanding of what the practice involves and gives you some experience of assisting in that process." If successful, there should be no shortage of work and you may find yourself in the middle of some of tomorrow's biggest legal issues. "One only has to turn on the TV or read the newspapers to see that environmental issues are of increasing importance. It's definitely a growth area."

*Pros:*

- Developing area of law, giving you the opportunity to be on the cutting edge.

- The excitement of leading a team into court.

- If you are passionate about our environment, this could be very rewarding work.

- Huge variety of work.

*Cons:*

- Lots of technical evidence.

- May have to spend years doing related areas until your practice is suffi-ciently developed to enable you to focus on the aspects that interest you.

*Ideas for Work Experience:*

- Spend time in the Planning or Environmental department of a Local Authority.

- Work in a relevant Government department such as DEFRA or the Environment Agency.

## European Law

Since the UK became a member of what is now the EU, European law (EU law) has had a significant impact on the law of England and Wales.

EU law is concerned with matters such as free trade which are regulated by EU Treaties but also relates to more social elements such as the free movement of persons. As with domestic law, EU law operates through legislation and common law and the interaction between domestic law and the new EU law lies at the heart of this practice area. "If issues of federalism and levels of different law interacting at a domestic and international level appeal to you, you may find it very interesting," says Maya Lester of Brick Court Chambers.

In theory at least, EU law takes precedence over national law and the European Court of Justice is the highest form of appellate court for England and Wales. Cases go to Europe either by way of appeal or as a complaint against a decision of the European Court or a piece of European legislation. Because of this overarching nature, EU law overlaps with literally every other area of law; in fact says Lester "it's not really an area of law at all but more a collection of legal provisions which crop up in a wide variety of cases". Chambers that specialise in EU law, and there are only a handful, also tend to focus their practice on competition, commercial and public law.

Despite the international aspect of EU law, "most of our time is spent in the UK" says Lester. While there is little oral advocacy at the junior end, you may be able to keep your skills ticking over through presentations for clients such as companies and regulators. However, in the early years at least, court work will be done by a barrister more senior than you.

The vital attribute of any EU lawyer is exceptional intellect. You will find "new things are being thrown at you all the time" says Lester. You will need to learn fast.

*Pros:*

- Intellectually stimulating.

- Potential for high-profile cases.

- Well paid.

- A fast-developing area of law.

*Cons:*

- Hearings are relatively infrequent.

- Very few chambers specialise in EU law so competition for pupillage is very tough and third sixes in the field can be hard to find.

*Ideas for Work Experience:*

- Work as a judicial assistant at the European Court of Justice in Luxembourg.

- Do a "stage" at the European Commission or the European Court of Justice.

- Learn another European language (note that French is the working language of the European courts so possibly the most helpful).

## Family

Family law covers a very broad spectrum of issues but is focused principally on the effects of the breakdown of a family relationship. At one extreme it includes an emergency application to move a child into Local Authority care; at the other extreme it could be arguing how many millions a pop star must pay an ex-spouse following a divorce. People's families are usually the most important thing in their lives, so separation, divorce and contact with children raise strong emotions. As a family law barrister you will deal with these issues and emotions on a daily basis. You may be the one who has to advise a father that a court is not going to allow him to see his teenage son, or a mother that she has lost custody of her new baby.

According to Rosie Budden of QEB, "excellent people skills are essential: there is often a very difficult personal dynamic involved in cases." An ability to inspire trust, to empathise and to communicate at your client's level is critical. However, you also need the common sense to see your client's legal case in isolation from the emotion surrounding it. "Your powers of persuasion must extend beyond persuading the judge and the other side. Often you will have to persuade your own client that what they are seeking just isn't fair or reasonable" says Budden. Richard Sear of 1 Hare Court agrees: "you need to be able to manage client expectations. With so many publicised big-money cases, there is a danger clients think they can get the same."

"The financial aspects of divorce law are constantly evolving," says Sear, "numbers are an important part and an interest in business matters certainly helps." Many cases settle before reaching court so you must have good negotiation skills along with the ability to see the big picture and understand what your client wants. Strategy plays a major role in some areas such as disputes between ex-spouses and child contact issues. Wherever the dispute has a financial aspect to it, "things can get very complex very quickly" says Sear.

There should be plenty of advocacy from the early years of practice. Expect around three or four court appearances each week. On top of that there will be conferences, drafting and liaising with solicitors. According to Budden, "every day is different, it's always interesting and no two cases are ever the same". You will encounter clients "from the broadest of backgrounds" says Budden and you must be prepared to help them without regard to their previous conduct.

If you are interested in family, be aware that "in this area, more than any other, mini-pupillages are vital" says Sear. The lower courts sit in private for family matters so as a member of the public you cannot watch any proceedings below the Court of Appeal: "to see the reality of the work at the junior end of the Family Law Bar you simply must do mini-pupillages."

*Pros:*

- Legally and factually very interesting—lots of variety in the issues and clients.

- You can make a real difference to people's lives.

- Lots of oral advocacy.

- Fast-moving and exciting area of law.

*Cons:*

- Emotionally draining—family barristers are reputedly the toughest at the Bar.

- Solicitor-advocates are appearing in court more frequently, reducing work at the Junior Bar.

*Ideas for Work Experience:*

- Mini-pupillages are essential.

- Anything which demonstrates you can put distressed people at ease and inspire confidence, whilst yourself remaining professional; work for the CAB or a helpline such as the Samaritans or Childline.

## Human Rights

The Human Rights Act 1998 effected a major injection of new jurispru-
dence into the law of England and Wales. Its provisions now impact upon
the practice of almost every area of the law. Moreover, the Act has struck
the public consciousness—it is politically sensitive as people become
more aware of their human rights and want them enforced.

"People say there's no such thing as a human rights barrister and
to some extent they're correct," says Alison Gerry of Doughty Street.
"Rather than specialising in human rights per se, junior barristers tend
to choose areas of law in which human rights issues will often come up."
Think education, prisons, employment, mental health, welfare, inquests
or immigration—anywhere, says Gerry, where "the individual is challenging the State". The unifying characteristic is the balancing of the
rights of an individual against the interests of society.

You will be faced with technical legal arguments and plenty of
advocacy from your first year of practice. However, you must show more
than intellectual and oral excellence to succeed here. Outstanding
interpersonal skills and "an ability to sympathise and empathise with
a client no matter who they are or what they've done" are essential.
"At the end of the day," says Gerry, "you're going to be affecting some-
body's life quite fundamentally." It is important that you are as comfortable dealing with a person who has spent their life in custody as you
are with the leader of a Local Education Authority or a school head
teacher.

Job satisfaction and intellectual stimulation can be very high—but
they come at a cost. Most of your clients will either be public bodies or
individuals funded by the Legal Services Commission (LSC). This means
you will be paid by tightly-budgeted public bodies and, at least for the
first few years, will probably earn substantially less than barristers
working in privately funded areas. Add to this the uncertainty surrounding
the way the Government is going to pay for legal services in the future
and, says Gerry, "it's all a bit scary at the moment. That said, if you
know you want to be a barrister and this is the area for you, do not be put
off." Azeem Suterwalla, also of Doughty Street Chambers agrees: "you
can earn a lot more at the Bar at sets that practise more commercial areas.
But it's not about the money—there has to be some deeper commitment
to the work."

*Pros:*

- Making a real difference to individuals who have often been let down by the system for their entire lives.

- Intellectually stimulating.

- Good balance of paperwork and oral advocacy.

- Fashionable growth area.

*Cons:*

- Earnings relatively low at the junior end.

- Building up a specialism can take many years.

*Ideas for Work Experience:*

- Work for an Non-Governmental Organisation (NGO).

- Work on death row, get involved with an Amnesty group or human rights charity.

- Work in a prison, a school or an immigration advice centre.

## Intellectual Property

In broad terms, intellectual property (IP) practitioners are concerned with protecting people's creations. Sometimes it will be the words of a book (remember the *Da Vinci Code* litigation?) or a section of a piece of music; at other times it could be the design for a new combine harvester or the formula for a cancer-controlling drug. The facts can vary dramatically but one thing draws them all together: one party wants to exercise a right over something to which another party asserts an exclusive claim.

The protection can be by copyright, patent, design right or trademark. As a junior practitioner, you should expect to do work that covers all four of these areas as well as associated areas such as confidential information. Typically you will be writing opinions, advising on points of law and practice, and drafting pleadings and skeleton arguments. Be prepared to wait a few years before regularly receiving instructions in your own right: the nature of IP cases tend to be such that you will spend most of your early years working as a Junior on more experienced barristers' files.

Consequently, although you may be in court up to 40 per cent of your time, you should not expect many opportunities for oral advocacy. Practice is "very heavily weighted in favour of paperwork" says Miles Copeland of Three New Square. Part of this paperwork will be legal research, an essential skill because of the "constant stream of new issues coming up and being debated" according to Kathryn Pickard of 11 South Square, "this makes it a very interesting area to practise in; the law is fascinating."

You can expect a varied client base and, often, genuine passion on the part of litigants. Your clients can be anyone from multinational pharmaceutical companies claiming infringement of a patent, to a folk band who is claiming that someone plagiarised their music. You must be able to treat all clients with professionalism, empathy and a clear understanding of their concerns and key interests.

Many come to the IP Bar with a scientific background. While not essential, this can put you at an advantage, particularly if your interest lies in patent law. Whether from a scientific background or not, a key skill is the ability to pick up a new set of facts very quickly: "you are constantly learning the detail of an entirely new subject matter" says Copeland.

*Pros:*

- Debates about key issues are very much alive.

- Intellectually stimulating.

- Endless variety of facts.

- Interesting client base.

*Cons:*

- Not many advocacy opportunities for the first few years.

- Long hours and lots of paperwork.

*Ideas for Work Experience:*

- Work in the Patent Office.

- Work for a large pharmaceutical company.

## Media

With a reputation for being one of the most glamorous areas of law, media law encompasses such areas as defamation, privacy, copyright and contract law. In practice this can mean everything from suing a magazine for defaming a celebrity client to advising on contracts or seeking an urgent interlocutory injunction to prevent the publication of unauthorised photos. Clients and cases can be extremely high profile (think the Beckhams or Catherine Zeta-Jones and Michael Douglas) and the work may take you into the world of sport, music, film or publishing.

Media law is fast-moving which, as Sara Mansoori of the Ministry of Justice, formerly of 5RB, points out, "gives practitioners the opportunity to make a real impact". There is a significant human element, especially in defamation practice, and, given the importance of understanding all the background facts to your case, you can find yourself learning about any number of surprising things, from a toxic waste spillage in the Ivory Coast to the intricate workings of a family business.

Following the introduction of the Civil Procedure Rules, more cases settle before reaching court. Mansoori says "lots of our battles are fought through paperwork". Day-to-day media practice will involve a mix of pre-publication and post-publication advice, pleading and injunction work with court appearances only on a sporadic basis at the junior end.

With all the celebrities and press attention, it is not surprising that media law has its glittery reputation. Be warned, however, that "while it can be quite glamorous, it's not as glamorous as everyone thinks" says Mansoori, "the reality is that you do a lot of work behind the scenes and it is the solicitor who has most of the contact with the client." However, with an exciting diet of interesting facts and interesting law, media law attracts a high number of candidates each year and the competition is tough.

*Pros:*

- Interesting facts, law and clients.

- Dynamic area of law where your cases can make an impact.

- Specialist area which makes it easier to keep up with developing case law.

- Because of the small size of the Media Bar, you will get to know the other barristers working in the field.

*Cons:*

- Long hours and concentrated spells of work, with few advocacy opportunities.

- Very few chambers specialise in media law so it can be extremely difficult to find a pupillage, and equally hard to find a third six.

*Ideas for Work Experience:*

- Work in media-related fields such as a newspaper legal office, television or radio station.

- Vacation scheme with a firm of solicitors specialising in media law.

- Journalism.

## Personal Injury

Personal Injury (PI) practice involves claims for compensation arising out of accidents that cause physical or psychiatric injury, or death. There is a broad spectrum of facts that can give rise to a claim—from the minor "trip and slip" cases to those where the claimant requires 24-hour care for the rest of their life.

The effect of this is that there is work for all levels of barrister. Andy Roy of 12 King's Bench Walk says that the practice of PI can be a good half-way house between criminal law and commercial—"you get a good mix of court work and paperwork with quite a lot of trial work and the opportunity to cross-examine". As well as oral advocacy from the beginning, your written skills and legal analysis will be tested. You can expect to be in court three or four times a week or more—"I am in court nearly every day" says Leila Benyounes of Park Lane Plowden. "In fact," continues Benyounes, "solicitors can be reluctant to give you work until they've seen you in court." At the junior end, factual issues usually determine a case's success, with technical legal points rarely raised. This changes as you become more senior and start having to combine an understanding of complex facts with a mastery of difficult legal principles.

Although the law may be similar in each case, the underlying facts are usually anything but. People are exposed to risk in almost every element of their lives and they can suffer an injury at any time. Claimants can be factory workers, school children, prisoners or hospital patients. This means you get a very real insight into different people's lives. You will also have to understand the background giving rise to the incident. This can mean becoming an expert in anything from car brake pads to making yoghurt pots. Even so, in the early years, practice can seem "a bit samey" says Roy because it will probably be dominated by minor road traffic accidents (RTAs).

You need intellect, advocacy and excellent interpersonal skills. Often, you will act for people at desperate times of their lives. Your performance may dictate whether they can have the care they need for life; part of the skill can be knowing when to accept a modest settlement and when to risk everything in court.

*Pros:*

- Lots of advocacy.

- Interesting facts.

- Variety in your client base.

- PI work is set to increase with society's movement towards being a "claim culture".

*Cons:*

- Practitioners have a reputation for being "ambulance chasers".

- Fast-paced, unpredictable lifestyle.

*Ideas for Work Experience:*

- Work in an insurance company or claims handling centre for an insurer.

- Work at your CAB or as a FRU social security rep.

## Planning

Planning is the area of law that controls the use and development of land. It draws on principles of property, contract, EU, judicial review and human rights law. Issues such as the extension of an airport terminal, the replacement of an old warehouse with a hypermarket or the construction of houses on a green belt are typical of the sorts of cases you will see.

An appeal from a planning decision (the stage at which counsel usually gets involved) will most commonly be heard in a specialist tribunal, meaning that most of your advocacy will be in front of an inspector rather than a judge. To be sure that locals can have their say, the tribunals will be held in the area of the proposed development so "you're often in a village hall rather than a courtroom" says Giles Cannock of Kings Chambers. This means that you will spend a lot of your time travelling throughout the country. On other occasions, you will appear in the High Court for the judicial review of a planning decision.

You can expect long hours and large amounts of detail to master. You must develop "the ability to read and absorb complex evidence very quickly" says Cannock. In addition, you must be able to "put together and manage a team" says Bridget Forster of No. 5 Chambers. Cases often have quite a big team of experts which you must co-ordinate—as counsel you will usually be responsible for ensuring the presentation of a united front between experts, solicitors and client.

Rewards come in the form of advocacy: expect to be on your feet regularly and dealing with important issues. Inevitably there is a tendency for planning cases to generate "an awful lot of paperwork", but after you've ploughed through the paper "you'll spend the whole time cross-examining expert witnesses" says Cannock: "it's a very pure form of advocacy". Forster agrees: "you can be cross-examining a noise expert one day and a newt expert the next".

*Pros:*

- Lots of high quality, contentious advocacy.

- Variety in types of law—contract, EU, human rights.

- Interesting facts.

- Cases will often give rise to great public interest and passion.

*Cons:*

- Travelling to Inquiries means time away from home.

- Lots of paperwork.

*Ideas for Work Experience:*

- Watch Planning Inquiries to understand how the dynamic differs from the courtroom.

- Work with a Local Authority in the Planning Department.
- Work with an architect or developer.

## Professional Negligence

All professionals owe responsibilities to their clients to provide a quality service and give good advice. Professional negligence (also known as professional liability) concerns the legal consequences of the situation where a client has suffered loss as a result of the mistake of a professional. The range of defendants can be very broad, including architects, engineers, bankers, accountants, solicitors and barristers. Whilst the duties owed by professionals are based on contract and tort, professional negligence practitioners also need to have a good grasp of many other areas of law, including trusts. Professional negligence involves "an interesting mix of fact, expertise and pure law" says Simon Myerson QC of St Paul's Chambers, Leeds and Byrom St Chambers, Manchester.

There has, over the last 20 years, been an increase in claims against professionals generally and therefore a significant growth in this area. As professionals should all be insured and therefore able to pay if a damages award is made against them, they may be the first person targeted when some aspect of a project goes wrong. As the parameters of the legal duties of professionals are still being defined, there are many interesting issues to be decided. All in all, "the volume of professional negligence litigation should continue to increase over the next few years" says George Spalton of 4 New Square.

As ever, excellent interpersonal skills are critical. If you act for the claimant there may be very strong emotions involved and perhaps even a general distrust of professionals. You must be able to put such clients at ease and inspire their confidence. If you are representing defendants there can be serious consequences if you lose: their livelihood could be at stake.

There is some small-scale professional negligence work for juniors in their first few years of practice, meaning, according to Spalton, that juniors are exposed to "much more advocacy and time in court than contemporaries at other commercial sets".

At some stage, junior tenants will be brought into larger, more complex cases, led by QCs. This provides an invaluable opportunity to learn—as well as to be involved in high-profile litigation.

In any event, whether acting on your own or in a team, it is essential that you can master large quantities of information quickly and understand how a small piece of information can cause the whole pond to ripple. "It really is the case that one sentence in a letter can change the entire expert's report or distinguish the case against you" says Myerson QC. For example, when judges must decide whether a professional gave the wrong advice, the details and circumstances of that advice will be crucial. You will also end up becoming an expert in whatever field the case concerns. Spalton observes, "One day you are dealing with a solicitor's advice to a corporate client about a complex commercial transaction and the next day an accountant's advice in relation to a tax matter."

*Pros:*

- Interesting factual situations.

- Often a great deal is at stake.

- An exciting stage for the development of the law and lots of work available.

- Exposure to a wide variety of professions, providing interesting work.

*Cons:*

- Increase in the number of cases settling at a late stage.

- Lots of law which can change bewilderingly quickly.

*Ideas for Work Experience:*

- Any work that brings you into contact with professionals—for example, working for an insurance company which provides professional liability cover.

- Any work in the office of another professional which is more than mere photocopying.

## Property Law

Many students assume the practice of property law (sometimes called "real estate"), to be unglamorous and uninteresting. "The reality," says Gwion Lewis of Landmark Chambers, "is very different." A person's home can be of great emotional and financial significance, meaning that on top of the intellectual stimulation of property law, there is "a huge amount of human interest involved".

The property practitioner will tackle issues arising from disputes about land and buildings, with a large part of the work made up of landlord and tenant disputes. At the junior level you can expect to appear in the County Court two or three times a week on relatively low-value matters such as possession actions, usually for rental arrears or against trespassers. You will also be in the Leasehold Valuation Tribunal (LVT), which, says Lewis, is "a dreadful name for what is in reality quite a straightforward institution". You must adapt your advocacy skills according to the forum. The LVT has very relaxed rules of evidence as it is a "process designed to be effective without advocates being there," so your approach will be very different from the higher courts. Lewis describes this as "a fantastic confidence building process", allowing you to improve and look towards more formal tribunals such as the High Court.

What does it take to succeed in property law? First, you must have an ability to analyse technical law: "even in the simplest matters there will be something that comes up that will require research," says Lewis. This drive to get to the right answer must be present both for the relatively straightforward cases and in the "fiendishly tough" (of which you can expect many). This academic ability must be balanced with a congeniality and empathy towards lay clients. Although the law and the institutions can look and sound dry, the factual disputes will be anything but. Everybody needs somewhere to live and clients are therefore surprisingly varied.

The combination of difficult, technical law and the clients' reliance on you can mean that even the simplest case takes a lot of work to prepare. Lewis warns "if you don't like stress, the Property Bar is probably not for you".

*Pros:*

- Lots of advocacy from the outset.
- Challenging and technical legal issues.
- Interesting clients with a great deal invested both emotionally and financially in their case.
- Can be very well paid.

*Cons:*

- Lots of research can mean very late nights in the library before a trial.

- A well-established area of law and not as fast-changing as some others.

*Ideas for Work Experience:*

- Working for a Local Authority in their housing department.

- Work for a housing charity such as Shelter or for the CAB advising on housing matters.

- Visit the LVT, County Courts and High Court to experience the issues and observe the different styles of advocacy at various levels.

## Public

"It's hard to give a one size fits all answer to the question: 'what is public law?' " says Tessa Hetherington of Matrix Chambers, "but essentially a public law practice is one dealing with cases involving governmental bodies and other public authorities acting in their public rather than private capacity." In simple terms, your time as a public lawyer will be spent either challenging or defending the decisions of public bodies.

The tension between the courts and politicians means that cases are often surrounded by intense public interest. European law also has a major impact and the level of scrutiny that the courts are to apply to decisions of public bodies continues to evolve—meaning that the law is constantly changing and you could have an effect on its development.

The primary mechanism of public law is judicial review in the High Court. The opportunities for advocacy on the high-profile cases are limited, warns Hetherington, "when you are very junior you may find that some solicitors are reluctant to send you straight up to appear in front of a High Court judge". That doesn't mean you won't be on your feet—within individual areas there are many opportunities for advocacy. Specialising in immigration, prisons or education, for example, will involve lots of oral advocacy in specialist tribunals.

To be a successful public lawyer "you need to think in a rigidly logical way" says Kathryn Perera of 11KBW; "you must construct an intellectually satisfying case for why something is right." This requires the ability to master large quantities of complicated facts as well as domestic legislation,

European legislation and any relevant guidelines or policy documents produced by the Government. But intellect is not enough; public law is a "sensitive area of practice that demands people skills" says Perera. According to Naina Patel of Blackstone Chambers, this means that "creativity and the ability to think outside the box" are essential: "in public law, more so than in more developed areas, you can be faced with the challenge of using existing authorities to support an entirely new legal proposition."

If you have the skills to be successful, it can be highly rewarding, as Hetherington explains: "because the cases are involved with the actions of Government and other public authorities they may have an impact on large numbers of people, meaning your work can be of great social importance." Patel agrees: "for me, it's about promoting Government accountability and the rule of law on a case-by-case basis."

*Pros:*

- Great sense of satisfaction, particularly if you win your client's case.

- It is rarely just money at stake, so you often feel as if you are doing something socially worthwhile.

- Cases can be high-profile and politically sensitive.

- Exciting, challenging area of law.

*Cons:*

- Lots of paperwork and sometimes cases are dry and technical.

- Remuneration does not reflect the apparent prestige of the work.

*Ideas for Work Experience:*

- Any work in a public body.

- Working for an MP or political think-tank.

- Any work that gives you a sense of how people live and how society functions.

**Tax**

"There is a misconception that tax law is all about numbers, accounting or tax returns. Actually it's not about that at all" says Hui Ling McCarthy of Gray's Inn Tax Chambers. To be a successful tax barrister, you require dynamism and creativity: it is about finding solutions to technical problems, often with many millions of pounds at stake. "Much of tax law is problem solving. It's work that you can really get your teeth into" says McCarthy. "You can go a long period of time without coming across the same question twice."

A junior tax barrister can expect their time to be split between before-the-event advice about how to minimise exposure to tax, and after-the-event advice about litigation. Although "it's not a complete advocacy desert" says James Rivett of Pump Court Tax Chambers, it may not be for you if you dream of oral advocacy. There are "phenomenally talented advocates" at the Tax Bar, says McCarthy, but as a junior the vast majority of your time will be spent at your desk. "Advisory work forms the bulk of your practice in the early years," she continues. What's more, your practice can be slow until you get yourself established: "you spend lots of time writing articles and chapters for books, or updating other texts" says McCarthy.

Tax practice is "very law-heavy" says Rivett—"you have to love the law to do this job". While it may seem that tax is a narrow field, in fact "there is a massive spectrum of different areas of law. This means that practice is incredibly broad: one day you will be arguing on the merits of a judicial review, the next on anti-dumping legislation or the taxation of shares and stock incentives, and the next day fraud."

Finally, a word of comfort for some: "You don't need to be highly numerate to practise tax law—although it helps if you can add up" says McCarthy.

*Pros:*

- So much is at stake financially that clients frequently appeal, meaning cases reach the higher courts quickly.

- Opportunities to write books and articles or lecture while your practice grows.

- Fewer last minute instructions—the complex nature of the work means that clients usually value quality over speed.

- Excellent financial prospects: tax barristers are the Bar's highest earners.

*Cons:*

- Very little oral advocacy for the first few years.

- Can take some time to establish your name and attract your own clients.

*Ideas for Work Experience:*

- Work with an accountant or auditor, or in the tax department of a solicitors' firm.

- Home study—Chartered Institute of Taxation exams (CTA) or Association of Tax Technicians (ATT) exams.

- Broader corporate or financial internships (for example, in an investment bank).

# SECTION 6:
# GETTING PUPILLAGE

The trick is to make a sparkling and dynamic impression in the written application, and then to make a deeper and more considered impact during the interview stage. That is of course easier said than done.

*Colin Wynter QC, Devereux Chambers*

# 21 APPLICATIONS

Filling out applications for pupillage is one of the most important things you will do in the course of your legal studies. If you have already completed a mini-pupillage at the chambers to which you are applying, take the opportunity to remind them why they should interview you. If you have not, this is your first chance to impress.

> Getting an interview is the most difficult bit. You have to distinguish yourself as having the 'X factor'. Be original.
>
> *Gwion Lewis, Landmark Chambers*

Students often forget the importance of an application form. With the constant stream of essays, coursework and exams, it is all too easy to put off an application form until the night before the deadline. Puzzling over the perfect syntax and searching for the best example to illustrate your abilities can be extraordinarily time-consuming. As a result, applications tend to take up far more time than you anticipate. Be sure to leave enough time to do yourself justice.

> *A Pupil*
> I started my applications long in advance but even so I only just got them all in on time. I would never have believed how long they took to get right—absolutely ages.

You will encounter three types of application:

- The Pupillage Portal (the Bar Council's online application system): an electronic form which can be sent to a maximum of twelve chambers subscribing to the system

- Non-Portal application forms: forms sent to individual chambers who do not subscribe to the Portal

- CV and covering letters

Check each chambers' website to see which application process they use.
Do not improvise your own.

> We get a few random have-a-go whimsical letters, some with photo-graphs attached. We have even had one scented application. These are my least favourite applications because it shows that the person can't be bothered to look us up; it shows that I shouldn't take them that seriously. They don't answer the questions that we are asking through the Portal that are designed to create a level playing field.
>
> *Barney Branston, 5 Essex Court*

It is absolutely crucial to give all your applications the time and effort that they deserve. While all three types of application should be completed with equal care, your Portal form will go to up to 12 chambers and you may therefore wish to invest correspondingly more time completing it. If you are focusing on a non-Portal form, it is also worth reading the Portal section of this chapter as there are many areas which will be applicable.

> I spent weeks honing my applications; I am glad that I did. You've got to take time over the form.
>
> *Richard Sear, 1 Hare Court*

### Before you start

Early in the academic year in which you are applying for pupillage, down-load all the available forms for the chambers in which you are interested. Ensure you do this well before the application deadlines begin (and for non-Portal sets, these get earlier every year as chambers try to pick off the top candidates first). Make a note in your diary of each date and set your-self reminders—deadlines have a nasty tendency to sneak up on you. Don't be one of the people who miss the deadlines and thus reduce their chances of getting pupillage.

Read through the downloaded forms carefully. Note any ideas you have for your answers and pay particular attention to any questions you do not feel able or ready to answer. Keep coming back to these questions to keep them fresh in your mind. You may find that an idea for an answer comes to you when you least expect it.

Through this preliminary reading, you may also identify gaps in your experience or CV that you should still have time to remedy. Can't think of an example when you have been in a position of responsibility? Sign up as class representative and start liaising between staff and students. Nothing to write in a question about mooting or debating? Enter a competition. If you read the forms early enough, you should be able to head off any potential areas of difficulty well in advance of the deadlines.

*How Many Applications?*

I applied for a lot—I think I had about a one in ten hit rate—ten applications per interview, and this was actually relatively high compared with many on my course.

*Alex Aldridge, journalist,* Legal Week

Send off as many applications as you can manage. At the time of going to press, the Portal gave you the option of 12 applications. Even if, initially, you think that there are only five chambers to which you would really like to go, it is worth applying to all 12. You may unexpectedly be impressed by a set during interviews or, equally, you may discover that you do not feel you fit in at your top choice. By applying to all 12, you can keep your options open. Remember that this is a highly competitive application process. It is an achievement to be among those candidates who get an interview with *any* chambers, let alone your first choice. Spread your applications over a spectrum of chambers in your field; do not simply apply for the top sets. Until you apply, you simply do not know how good you are. Theoretically, the more good applications you send out, the better your chances are of being invited for interview and thus your chances of getting pupillage.

*A Pupil*
With a mediocre 2:1, I thought it was unlikely that I was going to get a place in one of the best chambers. When it came to filling out my form I had a couple of spare places and applied to two chambers that I considered well out of my league—just on the off chance. My gamble paid off as, to my surprise, I was invited for interview. It was a huge boost to my confidence.

Outside the Portal there is no limit to the number of applications that you can submit. You should send off as many as you can complete within the time constraints and without sacrificing quality.

Make sure that you can still invest the required amount of time in each form. This means both time spent sitting down researching and drafting your answers but also time spent going out and getting the relevant experience to show that your interest in chambers' practice area is genuine. It is better to send off ten immaculate and tightly focused applications than 20 poorly written forms that fail to demonstrate a genuine interest.

None of this is to suggest that you should waste chambers' time by applying where you have no interest in their specialisms. Not only do you run the risk of irritating the barristers, your application is a waste of your own time in the unlikely event that you are offered a pupillage that you do not actually want.

*Criteria*

Every chambers is now required by the Bar Code of Conduct to prepare "a document setting out generally its policies in relation to the choice and number of pupils" which must be made available to all applicants. Check each chambers' website for the selection criteria before you start writing your applications. You should keep these criteria at the front of your mind as you are writing your applications.

The most common skills and aptitudes chambers are looking for include:

- Ability to relate to lay and professional clients.

- Advocacy skills.

- Analysis and reasoning.

- Determination.

- Interest in and commitment to areas of practice (legal work experience).

- Potential to make a positive contribution to chambers and its development.

- Proven academic ability (grades, scholarships and awards).

- Responsibility, leadership, teamwork.

- Well-developed oral communication skills.

- Well-developed written communication skills.

Beyond any specified criteria, remember that chambers are looking for applicants with the potential to be successful barristers.

*Referees*

You will have to provide at least one academic referee and usually a personal referee. Both are important. Before including someone as a referee, ask permission.

For your academic reference, not only do you need someone who will speak highly of you, but also they should be someone who knows you well enough to write your references and will do so promptly. A very common choice for an academic referee for those recently graduated from law school is a personal tutor. This is someone with whom you should have regular contact and who should have had a good overview of your work throughout the year. For those who graduated some time ago this can be more difficult; consider asking a BPTC tutor or speak to a careers adviser.

Avoid asking a tutor for whose classes you were perpetually late or from whom you always needed an extension. This advice holds true even if you achieved good grades. Equally, it may be futile asking your famous law lecturer whose name would hold considerable clout but to whom you were just another face in the lecture theatre. If you are going to ask your brilliant but scatty tutor, be prepared to chase them up. Make it your responsibility to check that references have been sent to chambers in time. Without references it is your application that will suffer.

You may also need a personal referee. If possible, ask a professional; this may carry more weight than someone who is just a friend.

> **Tip:** Give a copy of your application to your referees. This will act as a useful prompt for them as they write your reference and may help them to endorse your application more effectively.

Keep a good relationship with your referees. Do not forget to alert them in advance if they are likely to be asked for a reference, nor to keep them informed of how you fare.

*A Final Note Before You Begin*

Keep in mind that chambers want to get a feel for who you really are. Do not try to impress them with unnecessarily long words, Latin and legal jargon, nor interests or achievements which are not genuine.

> It's a hackneyed point but be yourself—there is absolutely no point in going to an interview pretending that you are absolutely fascinated by, say, anti-dumping measures if you are not, because you can bet your bottom dollar that one of the souls on the other side of the table will be fascinated and they will start interviewing you about it.
>
> *James Rivett, Pump Court Tax Chambers*

> Speak English: don't use eight syllable words if you don't need to.
>
> *Kevin Toomey, 2 Bedford Row*

Throughout your applications, avoid bald assertions: where possible, back up your answer with an example from your studies, work or other experience.

> The main things are substance and form. The key is to keep it as snappy as possible. The forms that stand out are those where very concise answers were given—where it's immediately clear what someone has done.
>
> *Kathryn Pickard, 11 South Square*

## The Three Types of Application

*The Pupillage Portal (formerly the OLPAS Form)*

A central application system for pupillages was set up by the Bar Council in 1996. Since then, it has had several incarnations: PACH (Pupillage Application Clearing House), OLPAS (the Online Pupillage Application System) and now, the Pupillage Portal. The Portal was launched in 2009 and can be found online at *www.pupillages.com*.

These online application systems have been the subject of much debate from both applicants and chambers over the years. As a result, the form has changed considerably and changes in future years are likely.

Nonetheless, the skills that are being assessed remain the same and the advice in this chapter is designed to apply to any new system, regardless of the exact manner in which questions are phrased.

The Portal gives you the opportunity to apply to twelve chambers and, if unsuccessful, to apply again to one chambers through a clearing process. The Portal opens around the middle of March each year, usually coinciding with the Pupillage Fair. First round applications close at the beginning of May. The interview season stretches across the summer with offers being made from around the beginning of August. Clearing opens in October.

> **Tip:** Give yourself plenty of time to get to grips with the Pupillage Portal website before you begin your applications. In past years it has not been entirely intuitive and you will benefit from spending some time exploring the site before completing your answers. In particular, ensure you are clear as to the exact point of time at which your form is submitted to chambers. In the past, many applicants have accidentally submitted their forms to chambers before they had finished reviewing them.

## Selecting Your Chambers

Before you begin completing your application form, compile the list of the twelve chambers to which you intend to apply. You must research each set thoroughly and ensure that their areas of practice match your experience so that you can demonstrate that your interest in them is genuine and informed. This process of researching chambers is surprisingly time-consuming.

> When you're looking for pupillage, you want somewhere that provides you with the opportunity to develop the practice that you want, but also somewhere that you're going to be happy and that feels like home. Your colleagues in chambers will be with you for the long haul; they will form the backbone of your professional life and among them you should find good friends. So choose a chambers where you can be yourself.
>
> *Naina Patel, Blackstone Chambers*

One word of warning when you are researching chambers: beware the "puff" on the website. Remember that while chambers' websites are invaluable for you, they are really aimed at solicitors and lay clients. This means that while a set may claim to have a "budding practice in environmental law", in fact this may mean that they have just one barrister who does the occasional case. If you then say that your real passion is environmental law, you may be met with several blank faces and headed straight for the rejection heap. Be careful. You can spot the "puff" by checking in the legal directories or asking your sponsor.

> Chambers write their own websites. Funnily enough all sets say they are brilliant. You must verify this by going and having a look either by mini-pupillage or reading Chambers and Partners.
>
> *Barney Branston, 5 Essex Court*

For most specialisms (tax being a notable exception), there may well be more than twelve contenders for the slots of your Portal form and you will need to give careful consideration to which ones you will eventually choose. It is wise to apply to a spectrum of chambers. Try to acquire a bit of self-knowledge and be realistic.

Opening Questions

The opening questions are straightforward and factual: name, address and educational history. Be honest about your actual grades and realistic about any predicted grades. If you are interviewed, it will probably be after you have had your results and it is likely that you will be asked for them.

Legal Work Experience

This is the section of the Portal where you can discuss your mini-pupillages, CAB or FRU work as well as other legal work experience, both paid and unpaid. Do not hesitate to include vacation schemes in this section. Chambers are likely to be impressed if you can show that your determination to become a barrister is based on a considered evaluation of the alternative option.

Previous versions of the online form have asked you to set out "details of your responsibilities or achievements" or to describe "what you learnt". Be specific and thoughtful when drafting your answers. Anyone can "attend court" or "observe a cross-examination"; did you learn the risk of asking a witness a question without knowing the answer? Did you learn an unusual method for drafting Defences or an effective new technique for undertaking research? Did you discuss with a barrister the possible approaches to a future case and start to learn about looking for flaws in a case theory?

That said, be careful not to oversell your learning.

*A BVC Student:*
On one mini I was with my mini-pupil supervisor as she left court and was interviewed by the media. When writing about this on my form, I blithely wrote that I had learnt how to deal with the press. Though unintentional, this was of course rather an exaggeration. While I had had my first brush with the media in a high-profile case, I would not know what to say to a hundred microphones pointing at me as I left court. When it came to interviews, I quickly realised my mistake . . .

Where you do include details of your experiences, it is a good technique to make descriptions active, rather than passive.

An effective way to explain what you learnt is to use the notes you made immediately after mini-pupillages (see Chapter 11). You can then choose a few of the most relevant examples to include.

Bear in mind that it is perfectly legitimate to be selective in the minis that you choose to write on your form. Always mention if you did a mini at a set to which you are applying, and any minis at sets which specialise in a similar field of law. This will show that your interest in this area is genuine. However, if you have spent two years doing criminal mini-pupillages, you do not need to mention them all—two or three will usually be sufficient.

Mention any minis where you saw really interesting cases or learnt something that you can discuss in a pupillage interview. Past minis are a frequent topic of interview questions so make sure you have picked the ones you can talk about.

If you found a particular mini was not a good experience and put you off an area of law, do not be afraid to say so on a pupillage application (after checking that none of the sets to which you are applying specialise in that area).

**One final point to note:** Be very careful not to breach any client confidentiality when writing about your work experience. This is particularly applicable to family law cases where even the names of the parties tend to be confidential. It also applies to other cases where reporting restrictions were imposed.

Non-Legal Work Experience

The advice above applies equally to the non-legal work experience section. This is also the section of the form where you can set out any previous employment history. One significant improvement of the Portal is that it gives those with first careers adequate space to discuss them.

Often included in this section are achievements arising from:

- Positions on a committee.
- Running your own business.
- International volunteer work.
- Charity or student welfare work.

Positions of Responsibility, Prizes and Awards

These sections of the form are largely self-explanatory. When describing any positions of responsibility, prizes or awards, do not feel that you need to use prose for your answers; bullet points or a simple list would be equally appropriate.

Interests and Recreational Activities

This section gives you space to show chambers that, as well as all the other attributes you have displayed, you are an interesting person whom they will want to have around chambers. This is one of the few places that you can use to stand out and you should make sure that you use it to full effect.

It is important for candidates to try and put themselves in the seat of the person who has got to read 200 forms; if you can, have something that makes you stand out.

*Sara Mansoori, Ministry of Justice, formerly at*
*5 Raymond Buildings*

Try to develop your hobbies or write about them in a more interesting light. For example, if you like reading, are you in a book group you could mention? If you enjoy travel, go further than simply listing the countries you have visited: mention something you learnt about another culture or an interesting experience (did you ride across Russia on a motorbike or learn the basics of sushi preparation in Japan?). If you coach football, could you talk about your five-a-side team's success in your local league?

If you have an interest that really sets you apart from the crowd, do not be afraid to mention it. Do you play the ukulele, go kitesurfing or know how to walk the tightrope? Hobbies that are a little bit different will attract chambers' attention.

> If you say you have an interest, have something to say about it when asked.
>
> *Leila Benyounes, Park Lane Plowden, Leeds*

One final word of advice: do not stretch your hobbies too far. If you declare a burning passion for something, it must be genuine. Sooner or later you will come up against someone on a panel who shares the same interest. This is a gift if you know your subject inside out, but a catastrophe if your embellishment is exposed. Do not run the risk. Honesty and integrity are paramount in this profession, as is the ability to substantiate everything that you say.

Monitoring Diversity

The Bar Council uses the online form to monitor the diversity of applicants. These sections are not passed on to chambers and are simply for the Bar Council's research purposes. All details are anonymised.

Mitigating Circumstances

In order to assess you fairly, it is important that chambers know of any circumstances which may affect how you appear as an applicant. These could include anything from a particular hardship you have suffered to an exceptional reason for any poor exam results or even the reasons behind a career break.

> If there were mitigating circumstances, we need to know what they were.
> It is difficult because those details tend to be very personal but we can't
> make an informed decision unless we know what the problem was.
>
> *Barney Branston, 5 Essex Court*

The Portal contains a section entitled "The Covering Letter". This can be
used to explain any such circumstances. Note that the section is designed
to enable applicants to include any information which is not covered elsewhere on the form. If you feel that you have covered everything, do not
feel obliged to use this opportunity.

There is some debate among pupillage committees as to whether it is
necessary to write your answer in the form of a formal letter. Ultimately
this is a matter for your own judgment and will depend on the wording
that the Bar Council use in their User Guide or in the preamble to the
section in the year that you apply.

Importantly, ensure that your referees are aware of any mitigating
circumstances, and ask that they address the issue if asked for a reference.

Questions about Your Motivation

This section of any application form tends to be the most difficult to
complete. You can develop the interesting details from your CV and
impress with your written advocacy but it is also easy to let yourself
down. It is such an important section that many pupillage committee
members reading the application forms will turn to it first.

> **Tip:** Whatever the stated word limit (and these have fluctuated significantly
> in recent years), it is absolutely essential that you remember this is a *limit*
> and not a *target*. Do not be afraid to keep your answers considerably shorter
> than the limits set. Aim to be concise and pithy. Chambers receive literally
> hundreds of applications each year; they are less likely to read your form
> thoroughly if it is unnecessarily long.

In the past this section was the only part which could be customised to
each chambers and it is likely that this custom will remain. If it does,
make sure that you take full advantage of this opportunity and tailor your
experiences so as to demonstrate to chambers that you are the perfect
candidate for them.

**Why do you wish to become a barrister?** This is probably the most important question to get right and it is essential that you have a polished answer.

Chambers are looking for:

- An understanding of the profession.

- Evidence that you have made a commitment to the Bar.

- Evidence of an ability and interest in advocacy.

- Interest in the law itself.

- A desire to be self-employed.

If your answer does not demonstrate some of the above criteria, your application is unlikely to make it through the first round.

A couple of the things which I've particularly enjoyed about being a barrister are the independence of the profession and the freedom and control over your own destiny which being self-employed allows. I've also loved the advocacy and dealing with a whole cross-section of different people's issues and problems and being able to get your teeth stuck into a problem and then see it right through to the end of a court hearing.

*Tim Kevan, barrister and author of* BabyBarista and the Art of War
(Bloomsbury 2009)

One way to approach this question is to draw up a list of every reason why you would like to become a barrister. Include all the reasons that may sound mediocre or self-serving (you may later think of an angle from which these actually fit into the criteria above). Now think about all the reasons why *anyone* might consider being a barrister (even if at first you think that these do not apply to you) and add all the positive points that you think the profession has to offer. By approaching the question in this way, you might come up with some reasons which are applicable to you but which you might otherwise have overlooked.

Now divide your list into those factors which you think will interest chambers and those which will not. Cross off anything which does not apply to you. This final list probably provides more than enough material for an answer. Should you find this not to be the case, have a look at Chapters 1 and 2. If you still feel uninspired, you might want to reassess your career choice . . .

When it comes to writing up your answer, try to tie in your reasons with your own experiences. Not only is it far more impressive to demonstrate that your desire to practise at the Bar is borne of experience, it will help your answer to stand out from all the generic answers which chambers receive. There are only a limited number of reasons you can give for wishing to be a barrister so use examples to show chambers that you have something extra and that you are making an informed choice.

Your Preferred Areas of Law

Chambers generally try to identify not simply the best candidates but more specifically the best candidates for the work undertaken by the particular chambers. If your stated interests lie in areas of work not undertaken by the chambers to which you have applied, your application may be wasted.

*Colin Wynter QC, Devereux Chambers*

You must invest a great deal of time researching the areas of practice of each chambers to which you are going to apply. This should be done before you begin to fill out this answer. Each set wants to see that you are interested in the areas of law that it practises—do not fail to demonstrate this commitment.

Really, really tailor your application to the areas you wish to practise.
*Kevin Toomey, 2 Bedford Row*

If these sections are really quite generic it looks as if your applications are unfocused.

*Richard Sear, 1 Hare Court*

Where people are over-general on an application, it betrays that they aren't really focused on any of the areas listed – they are hedging their bets. This may be fine for the general common law chambers but, for those with specialisms, you are much better targeting one area.

*James Rivett, Pump Court Tax Chambers*

Think about why you wish to practise in your chosen fields. If you are lacking inspiration, try re-reading Chapter 20 on selecting your practice areas or refer to the pupillage listings handbooks.

*A Pupillage Committee Member:*
It sounds obvious to say "make sure you mention chambers' main practice area if you are going to apply" but every year applicants fail to do so. My chambers is extremely specialised and yet amazingly the vast majority of applicants do not mention our speciality. Of those that do, literally only a handful have any relevant experience to support their claim that they wish to practise it. Whenever I come across a form which expresses an interest in what we do and shows some evidence that this interest is genuine, I am strongly inclined to put that form into the "yes" pile. Each year I hear so many applicants complaining that they don't get interviews but each year I read so many forms which make this most basic mistake.

Reasons for your Choice of Chambers

Your answer to this question will be sent separately to each set to which you apply. You are therefore able to write a specific answer for each chambers to which you are applying. Use this opportunity to identify particular features of each set that appeal to you.

Researching and explaining this requires considerable thought. Look at each set separately, spend some time on each website and look in the legal directories. A common error is to use one generic answer and to send it to all twelve chambers saying, for example, "I have applied to a range of general common law chambers because. . ." as opposed to saying "I have applied to Denning Chambers because. . .". Avoid making this mistake.

You may find that most of your reasons are applicable to more than one chambers. Despite this, show that you have gone to the effort of writing an individual answer. This is far easier if you have undertaken a mini at the set: you will be able to discuss some of the things you picked up during your week. If you have not done a mini, try to include at least one thing which is specific to each chambers; for example, this could be a case you have read, a barrister you saw in court or an aspect of their pupillage programme.

We had one applicant who said chambers' chancery reputation goes without saying. It does because nobody's ever said it.

*Andy Roy, 12 King's Bench Walk*

Include chambers' name—and make sure it is the right chambers' name:

*A Pupil:*

Reading back over my form I realised I had accidentally put one chambers' name into another's section. It was too late to change it. Whoops.

It is also worth remembering that this section is an opportunity to sell yourself as a candidate. Again, tie your interest in chambers to your own experience.

Your Expectations of Life in Chambers

If you are asked questions about your expectations, be aware that pitching the answers at the appropriate level can be difficult. There may be no right answer, but there are a myriad of wrong ones. While you may well go on to dazzle chambers with your legal knowledge and advocacy ability, at the time of completing your form you are an unknown quantity.

In order to avoid any of the potential pitfalls, think about what the chambers you are applying to has to offer. Consider their pupillage scheme: how many supervisors will you have and how will this benefit you? Will you be on your feet in the second six? Does chambers offer a broad pupillage with the chance to experience a range of practices or will you specialise early on? Think about your own practical experience and which aspects of it you hope to develop during pupillage and give reasons. Think about life at the junior end of your chambers and what you would like to get out of it. For an insight into the realities of life at the junior Bar, have a look at Adam Kramer's *Bewigged and Bewildered* (Hart Publishing: 2007).

Chambers are seeking to make an investment in their pupils. They are looking for someone who will not only do the work well and with good cheer but who will eventually attract work themselves. To demonstrate that you have the necessary skills and determination to succeed in chambers, try using concise examples.

Given how difficult such questions are, you would probably also be well-advised to keep any answers short.

**Final Portal Tip:** Try to submit your form well before the deadline. In past years the system has crashed in the final 24 hours, causing some applicants to miss the deadline. If you do find yourself in the unlucky position of having been unable to send off your form due to a technical difficulty, contact the Portal administrators: in previous years the system has been re-opened.

## *Non-Portal Applications*

Numerous chambers have their own application forms and choose not to use the Portal. This can be for any number of reasons, from wanting to catch the top applicants before the Portal season begins, through to a desire to ask a different range of questions of their applicants. There should be no inferences drawn if a chambers in which you are interested does not subscribe to the Portal.

Most non-Portal application forms will in fact be similar to the Portal form, especially since it has been extended, so be sure to read the Portal advice above. There are however a number of different questions that repeatedly come up on non-Portal forms.

### Detailed Breakdown of Grades

One common requirement on non-Portal forms is a more detailed break-down of your degree or GDL grades. There is no way around this. If you fear that your grades are not suitably impressive, the only thing you can do (unless you have serious extenuating circumstances) is dazzle chambers with the rest of your form.

If you don't have a First, think about how much detail to include when declaring your grades. One school of thought is that you should try to show your grades in their best light: if you are predicted a 2:1 for your overall degree but got a First in your land law coursework, say so.

*A Pupil*
I was advised to emphasise my academic credentials as much as possible on my form as I only got a 2:1. I gave plenty of details: how close I was to a First, where I'd done particularly well in any papers, the scholarship I'd got at university–even my GCSE results. It worked–one chambers told me they were worried I was too academic for the job.

Others, however, think this gives the impression that you are making excuses for yourself or trying to inflate grades that are simply not good enough.

There is no consensus. Ask your sponsor and exercise your own judgment.

Demonstration of Your Written Ability

Another common feature of a non-Portal form is that it will often ask to see some demonstration of your written skills. This can range from asking you to write about your work experience, some past achievement or a short argument on a point that interests you. With such questions, several skills are being assessed: your persuasiveness; your ability to write succinctly but effectively; and your judgment in choosing the topic you elect to write about.

Ensure that if a word limit is given you do not exceed it. Chambers want to see that, when necessary, you can keep your answers short. Avoid writing in minute script in order to squeeze in every last word.

One of the skills that is being assessed is the ability to present information clearly. If you must handwrite a form, remember to write legibly.
*Wendy Hutson, Adult Careers Adviser*

If you have a choice about what to write for a question of this nature, err on the side of caution. Even if chambers explicitly states that your answer can be humorous, be careful about making any sort of joke. What seems hilarious to you at the time of writing may not go down so well with the reader.

You may be required to address a legal problem on an application form. Should this be the case, approach it as you would a piece of coursework. Dedicate enough time to thorough research and write your answer with care. For more information on tackling legal problems, see Chapter 22.

Mini-Pupillages

A non-Portal form may require you to list all your mini-pupillages (unlike the Portal form on which you can be selective). If this is the case, do so.

*The Pupillage CV and Covering Letter*

The Pupillage CV

The pupillage CV should be a maximum of two A4 sides. It should be focused on those experiences which show that you have the requisite skills to be a successful barrister. If you need advice on how to write a CV from scratch, there are several good books and websites available. In addition, your local careers service should be able to provide expert guidance. This section will suggest ways to redraft a CV into a more desirable form.

First, check that your CV already covers the main areas that are expected of a CV and add any that are missing:

- Name and contact details including landline number, mobile number and email address.

- Education details including where you studied and what grades you received (in reverse chronological order).

- Details of any previous careers.

- Work experience, legal and otherwise, paid and unpaid (again in reverse chronological order).

- Any achievements or scholarships.

- Any languages.

- Contact details for at least one, and ideally two, referees.

You could use this list as a guide to the way you wish to order your pupillage CV, but as long as your contact details come first, it is simply a matter of taste.

When writing a pupillage CV, separate your legal experience from your non-legal experience. Go through all your legal work experience (including mini-pupillages and vacation schemes) and make a list of all the things that you learnt (as described above for the Portal work experience section).

**Tip:** Instead of writing out these lists in detailed, immaculate prose, you could write them as succinct bulleted lists and add them below the corresponding work experience.

You should not dismiss non-legal work unless it really is irrelevant and does not demonstrate a skill that might be valuable to your life at the Bar. For example, if you have worked as a waiter or waitress for three years to put yourself through your degree, consider keeping it in. Does it show your determination to be a barrister as well as staying power, people skills and the ability to multi-task? If you did a job that does not lend itself to displaying any such qualities, you might want to leave it out.

Now double-check everything and make sure that it sits well on the page—not too squashed together and not so spread out that it looks empty. You can use bullet points, sub-headings and bold or underlined script to help with this. Select a plain font (Arial or Times New Roman) and make sure that it is a sensible size so that your reader does not have to get out a magnifying glass.

Finally, take your CV to your careers department or local careers service and ask them to have a look. Ask a friend (preferably a law colleague) to read it too. A fresh pair of eyes will often be able to spot minor mistakes that you have overlooked or suggest areas where you can tighten up the wording or make more of your achievements. You do not have to feel bound by suggestions from others; they are after all simply suggestions and it is more important to retain the individuality of your CV than to follow to the letter all the advice you receive. Use your common sense.

The three watchwords for CVs are relevance, evidence and proportions. Which of your skills and achievements are most relevant to the reader's interests? Provide evidence (never just claims) that you have these skills, and in proportions that match the reader's order of priority. Your interpersonal skills are essential to success as a barrister, but a section about them should not take up eight lines if only three lines are devoted to advocacy. Headings are important: they should draw the reader's attention by relating to their interests. If you are captain of a university sports team, rather than a section headed 'Sports', put this information under, for example, 'Leadership' or 'Communication' or 'Organisation' or 'Teamwork'.

*Dr Ruth Smith, Cambridge University Careers Service*

The Covering Letter

> An outstanding CV will demonstrate exceptional talent; an outstanding
> covering letter, exceptional drive.
>
> *Hui Ling McCarthy, Gray's Inn Tax Chambers*

Be careful not to put all your effort into your CV and rush off a quick
covering letter.

As with mini-pupillage applications, there are two questions which you
need to answer in a covering letter to chambers: why you and why me?
Demonstrate that you have researched chambers fully, that your interest
in their practice is genuine and that your letter is not a cut-and-paste job
of all the letters you have sent to other chambers.

When writing about yourself, pull out a few of the highlights from your
CV and develop them. Discuss any particular experience or success which
makes you an attractive candidate and demonstrate your interest in chambers and its practice areas. Examples could be a mini-pupillage you
undertook with them or a similar set, a relevant option course you took or
a competition where you mooted on a subject in which they specialise.

In almost all cases, be sure to stay within one side of A4. You may go
onto a second page if you are required to handwrite your letter (your
writing will almost certainly be larger than typed script), or if you are
applying to a specialist chambers in a niche area of law such as tax or
intellectual property. In this case, it can be worth going over a page in
order to demonstrate your interest in their field. Be specific about what
interests you and why, and do not be afraid to go into details of your
experience.

Set out your letter correctly and, as usual, check for spelling and grammatical errors. Print the letter and CV on regular white A4 paper–no lined
paper torn from a note pad and no notelets.

### Check, Double-Check, Proofread, Second Opinion, Edit and Check Again

Do not send off any application unless you have checked it yourself at
least twice and, if it is typed, run it through a spell check. Be particularly
wary of any words that have been auto-corrected: "tortious" not
"tortuous"! Try to persuade a family member or friend to double-check it.

Chambers receive literally hundreds of application forms each year and some chambers will automatically discard any application with even a single spelling mistake or grammatical error. After you have checked your application, leave it overnight (or longer if possible) and give it a thorough final check before you submit it; a night's sleep may give you a little more distance and thus objectivity with which to spot mistakes.

What really fails to impress are typos. This is a critical document and it's vital that you present it accurately—you are trying to launch your career at the Bar. Presentation and spelling are really important; your application demonstrates how you will present work further down the line. A document with mistakes is not something you would want to send out to instructing solicitors or to be read by the court.

*Sara Mansoori, Ministry of Justice, formerly of 5 Raymond Buildings*

As well as checking the body of your application, check your name, address, phone number and email. It is amazing how many people leave errors either because they assume they could not have got these wrong or because they change address and phone number and forget to update their details.

*Wendy Hutson, Adult Careers Adviser*

**Tip:** Before you begin to send out your applications, check the greeting on your answer phone. Chambers may telephone to invite you for an interview and they may not be amused by a comedy message.

Do not be too disheartened if you do not receive a single offer of interview after your first round of applications. This is not uncommon. Review your application strategy, identify your weaknesses and devote the next few months to improving your CV. Take heart: many candidates who eventually get pupillage are applying for the second, third or fourth time.

# 22 INTERVIEWS

Reaching the interview stage is an enormous achievement.

Too many barristers look back on their very first interview a "the sacrificial interview" where they did not know enough to perform well. This was not helped by the fact that, until recently, the interview process was shrouded in mystery; there was very little information available telling candidates what to expect. This is no longer the case. Chambers' websites now explain the process and barristers offer insider expertise at lectures organised by the Inns and law schools.

That said, pupillage interviews are some of the most gruelling you will ever face. It will always remain impossible to anticipate exactly which questions will arise and to pinpoint specifically what the panel are looking for. Nevertheless, if you have been called for interview, careful research, preparation and practice can dramatically influence the result and you could walk away with that elusive pupillage.

The aims of this chapter are:

- to outline some of the different formats of interviews;
- to explain how to prepare for them;
- to give you an insight into what you might expect once through the door of an interview;
- to identify the seven specific types of questions usually asked at pupillage interviews;
- to explain what the panel is looking for when they ask questions;
- to suggest some approaches to answering them;
- to explain how to use mock interviews; and
- to offer some final words of advice before you walk through the interview door.

## What to Expect in a Pupillage Interview

Chambers' procedures vary dramatically. Pupillage interviews can be anything from one round to two or even three rounds. The selection process may include a compulsory mini-pupillage, an advocacy exercise, a case-study or a moot.

*Single Round Interviews*

Interviews can be one round for numerous reasons and it is not in any way an indication of the calibre of chambers or the effort they invest in their pupils.

Make sure you know, when walking into the interview, whether it is the only round—if so, you have less time to impress.

*A Pupil*

I went to one interview wrongly thinking it was the first round of two. As a result I made less effort to turn on the hard sell and promote myself. I didn't mention the scholarship I had recently been awarded as I thought I would 'keep it up my sleeve' to impress them in round two. This turned out to be a big mistake—there was no round two.

Always go into an interview firing from all barrels and never keep anything back. You may not get that second chance.

Unsurprisingly, single round interviews tend to be a combination of the first and second round interviews described below. You can expect to be grilled on your application, on your views and you may be presented with some form of legal problem. Make sure you are fully prepared for whatever occurs.

*Multi-Round Interviews*

Usually, where chambers has more than one round of interviews, the first round is shorter, less formal and more general. Some barristers see first round interviews as an opportunity "just to check the candidates are human". First round panels tend to have between two and five interviewers who may be more junior than second or third round panels.

Where there is more than one round, first round interviews tend to last between 10 and 30 minutes and questions often focus on the candidate's application form, opinions and motivation rather than delving deeply into their knowledge of the law.

First-round interviews are usually fairly short; perhaps no longer than 15 minutes. There is no time to unearth a candidate's deeper qualities. Impressions are key. Consider how to create a series of favourable impressions. So, for example, walk into the room with confidence, maintain eye contact and, if you can and the occasion allows, smile.

*Colin Wynter QC, Devereux Chambers*

In some interviews, the panel may tell you how many people they are interviewing, how many places there are in the next round and when you can expect to hear back. Do not read anything into this: all candidates will be given the same information so being told the date of round two is not a hint that you have made the grade.

After the first round, the number of candidates will be reduced significantly. This process usually happens fairly quickly and you can expect to be recalled or rejected within a few weeks. If you do not hear anything you might be on a waiting list—do not give up hope until you receive a rejection letter. If you do not hear anything after three weeks, it can be worthwhile calling chambers and politely enquiring about the status of your application.

Second and third round interviews tend to be longer, more rigorous and in front of a larger and more senior panel. If you are going to be asked a legal problem question it will probably be in the final round and you will often be given a period of time (anything from two weeks to ten minutes) to prepare.

Although second and third round interviews are likely to be nerve-wracking, do not forget that your chances of success are much higher by this point. Chambers will have received hundreds of applications and you are now down to the final group. Even if you do not make the final cut, this is a huge achievement in itself. Remember: if you are good enough to have reached a second round anywhere, you should be good enough to get pupillage somewhere.

## What Chambers are Looking for in Interview Candidates

Poise and the ability to engage.

*Michael Mylonas, 3 Serjeants' Inn*

Stickers, not quitters—people who will stay the course, not those who see the Bar simply as a springboard to other things.

*Hui Ling McCarthy, Gray's Inn Tax Chambers*

Good presentation, engaging with the interviewers, listening to and answering the questions. We look for someone with whom we would be happy to spend time in chambers.

*Andy Roy, 12 King's Bench Walk*

Academic excellence and clarity of thought.

*James Duffy, Fountain Court*

The ability to answer the question posed. Pause, reflect and weigh up the answer, then give a well-reasoned answer that comes down on one side.

*Sara Mansoori, Ministry of Justice, formerly of 5RB*

People who are confident, engaging, have a sense of humour and leave an impression.

*Azeem Suterwalla, Doughty Street Chambers*

The ability to relate to people—soft skills—combined with hard skills of intellectual ability.

*Tessa Hetherington, Matrix Chambers*

Applicants who are composed, well-presented, bright, conversant and socially able.

*Ruth Holtham, Serle Court*

We are looking for high academic standard and evidence that you haven't lived in a box.

*John Furber QC, Wilberforce Chambers*

Common Mistakes:

One of the biggest mistakes we see in first round interviews is when we challenge someone on a point of view and they are unable to maintain their argument. It is common to see candidates flip-flop between what they were arguing about. They forget that the point of these interviews is to see if they can argue a case.

*James Duffy, Fountain Court*

The worst scenario is when people freeze and can't talk.

*Michael Mylonas, 3 Serjeants' Inn*

Not answering the question. Some people have things they are determined to mention so they will crow bar something in without being asked.

*Andy Roy, 12 King's Bench Walk*

When challenged on a technical point, it is incredible how many interviewees give a half-hearted answer ending with, '. . . but you probably know about that better than me'. If it's intended to be flattering, it isn't. We know the correct answer, or at the very least we certainly like to think we do. The point of the question is to discover your answer, especially if you have professed a particular interest in the area. We certainly don't know that better than you.

*Hui Ling McCarthy, Gray's Inn Tax Chambers*

Pomposity. Also we are not impressed by people with no backbone—we want people who can argue their side, who do not give up when challenged but equally who have the confidence to admit it when they don't know.

*Kevin Toomey, 2 Bedford Row*

## Types of Questions

Pupillage interviews generally consist of seven types of questions:

1. Why you want to be a barrister.

2. Why you want to work in a certain area of law.

3. Why you applied to this chambers.

4. Questions about your application and personality.

5. Ethical dilemmas.

6. Current affairs questions.

7. Legal problems.

These are addressed in turn below.

*1. Questions about why you want to be a barrister*

What chambers are looking for:

- An understanding of the profession.

- Evidence that you have made a commitment to the Bar.

- Evidence of an ability and interest in advocacy.

- An interest in the law itself.

It's always the first question you're asked: why do you want to be a barrister and why this chambers?

*George Spalton, 4 New Square*

This question, in some form, is almost guaranteed to come up. The reason is obvious. Pupillage will be a demanding start to a tough career. Chambers want pupils with determination and a commitment to the profession that will carry them through the inevitable late nights and early mornings—not pupils who will crumble under the pressure and run off to another profession.

It is easy to make the mistake of thinking that a desire to be a barrister will be a given. For this reason some candidates don't think about what their answer will be and their chances of success suffer.

*A Pupil*
When I was applying during my final year at university, I stumbled over my answer. One of the panel asked me 'If you don't know why you want to be a barrister, why are you here?'. It was horrible. I spent the following year sorting myself out and did better the next time around.

Remember that you will most likely have answered this question in your written application. Consistency is vital. Check what you wrote and use that as a foundation for a new list of all the reasons why you want to be a barrister. Your list may look like a string of clichés. If this is the case, try to think of interesting ways to express them. The easiest and most effective way to do this is to tie the abstract reason ("I enjoy advocacy") to a specific physical event or experience ("I took part in five moots this year and won four of them"). Always relate your answer back to your experiences in some way. Not only will this bring your answer to life and make it different from everyone else's but you will also have the chance to highlight some aspect of your CV which might impress the panel.

This question is so common that you should have your answer clearly arranged in your head. In advance, practise it aloud several times. Ask someone you live with to ask you this question regularly (and when you are not expecting it) and each time spend a minute telling them your answer. Try to answer conversationally rather than giving a formal, scripted answer. By doing this, you should cement the key points you want to make without running the risk that your answer will sound over-prepared in the interview itself.

Finally, make a list of all the reasons why you do not want to be a solicitor. If you have had the advantage of having worked for a solicitors' firm, draw on this experience. Be positive about the Bar rather than negative about solicitors; remember you will be working closely with (and reliant on) solicitors throughout your career.

There are questions in interview that you cannot anticipate. But most questions in interview are ones that you really ought to have thought about before, such as 'Why are you pursuing a career in the law?' It's very telling if an applicant appears to be thinking about those questions for the first time. You shouldn't be in the interview unless you have thought quite hard about those questions before the interview. It's easy to distinguish someone who has thought quite hard about those questions from someone who's thinking about them for the first time.

*Richard Wald, 39 Essex Street*

*2. Questions about why you have applied to this chambers in particular*

What chambers are looking for:

- An understanding of chambers' practice areas.

- An appreciation of the quality of work in chambers.

- An understanding of the atmosphere in chambers.

- Knowledge of what pupillage in that chambers involves (for example whether they encourage you to take on your own cases in the second six).

This question is most easily answered if you have the experience of a mini-pupillage at the set. If so, revise the cases you saw and the barristers' names and this question should pose you no problems.

If you don't have the experience of having done a mini-pupillage at the set, do not panic. You will just have to do a little more work to be able to give a convincing answer. You need to research the chambers thoroughly. Read every bit of literature about them that you can. Browse their websites, read their write-ups in the pupillage handbooks (see Chapter 29 on Resources) and read what the *Legal 500* and *Chambers and Partners* say about them. Re-read any literature they may have given you at the Pupillage Fair or a chambers' evening. If you have a friend who did a mini with them, ask them how chambers views themselves and for any other details they picked up.

Try to get a flavour of chambers' actual practice. If chambers' website mentions a recent case, read it. Even better, if it made the headlines, read what the papers had to say about it and make sure that you have your own opinion on it. If anyone from the set was involved in any of the major cases that you have encountered on your legal studies, read them and, again, form an opinion. Aim for specifics: it is much more impressive to answer the question with detail than with general statements.

List all the areas of practice that chambers offers and make sure that you consult your list just before your interview. It is often the case that you have the websites of several chambers whirling round in your head. It is disastrous if you cannot remember which is which, and mistakenly declare your passion for an area in which they do not practise.

*3. Questions about why you want to practise in a particular area of law*

What chambers are looking for:

- A genuine interest in chambers' practice areas (particularly any areas that might be growing).

- An understanding of what those areas of law entail in practice.

- Evidence that you have the requisite skills to be successful in those areas.

Answers to this question usually consist of two parts: why you like the academic area of law and why you like its practical application.

Think back to when you were choosing the area of law in which you wanted to practise (see Chapter 20). Recall the reasons you made these choices. When you have done this, think of specific experiences to support your answers. Mini-pupillages, pro bono work or relevant experiences from previous jobs can all be excellent illustrations of your point.

Before your interview, check chambers' specialisms again and remember them when asked this question. If chambers is famed for a particular area, bear in mind that you should at least acknowledge your awareness of this, even if it is the set's other areas of practice which really appeal to you. Take care: chambers may be reluctant to award pupillage to a candidate whose interests do not match chambers' practice.

## 4. Questions about your application and personality

What chambers are looking for:

- Oral consistency with your written profile.

- Eloquence when discussing topics with which you are familiar.

- Ability to explain concepts or tell a story.

- Ability to identify strengths and weaknesses in your own character.

- Whether you would "fit in" in chambers.

Your written application is usually all the panel will know about you before you walk in.

You probably sent off your application in April and it is likely to be June or even July before you set foot inside chambers. It sounds obvious but it is easy to forget what you wrote: re-read your application before you go to the interview. As you read it, think about the answers you have given and the areas of your form on which they might question you. Is there anything interesting or unusual about your form? If so, it is likely to come up at interview.

Remember that you must be able to speak in detail about everything you wrote. The interviewers posing the questions are experts in cross-examination. Barristers are trained to spot loop-holes and lies.

Never exaggerate or bluff—they will see straight through you and will keep asking questions until you hit a brick wall. Do you recall the cases that you came across on your mini-pupillages? Look them up. If any cases have been reported, read the judgments and ask yourself if you agree with the result. Think of something intelligent to say about such cases so that you can impress the panel if they ask you about them. Remind yourself of the names of every barrister you met on your mini-pupillages. Research them on chambers' websites, discover the areas in which they specialise and look up the recent cases in which they have been involved.

> **Tip:** Barristers, particularly senior barristers, tend to know other sets by the name of the head of chambers rather than chambers' name itself. Memorise the heads of chambers for each set you have been to in case you are asked.

Interviews are intended to judge further the intelligence and articulacy of the candidate. Many people who are very well qualified in law prove to be disappointing in the flesh.

*John Furber QC, Wilberforce Chambers*

Think about the common questions that everyone knows are asked at interviews. What makes you laugh? What books have you read recently? Think about trying to explain any deficiencies on your CV. Think about questions you can ask those interviewing you.

*Miles Copeland, Three New Square*

Also in this category are the miscellaneous questions aimed at finding out about you personally. These are designed to see whether you will fit into chambers and whether you can think on your feet. These questions vary from the relatively bland (what is your favourite film?) to the ridiculous (if you were a cartoon character, who would you be and why?).

There is very little you can do in the way of preparation for such questions. When they are thrown at you, take a moment to consider, then try to answer as intelligently as possible. Treat them seriously even if they appear absurd. If you feel confident using humour then do so. Beware, however, that flippancy or an inappropriate joke can destroy your chances of success.

**Examples of some standard questions:**

- Why do you think you would suit our chambers?

- If you could invite three people from history or the present to dinner, whom would you invite and why?

- What is your greatest achievement?

- What is your greatest failure?

- What do you think is your most serious character weakness?

- Spend two minutes convincing us of something you feel passionately about

- Why didn't you read law at university?

- How would your friends describe you in three words?

- What are you planning to do between doing your BPTC and starting pupillage?

## 5. Ethical dilemmas

What chambers are looking for:

- Evidence that you have good judgment and common sense.

- Proof that you understand that your duty to the court supersedes your duty to your client, and your own career advancement.

- Evidence that you have the confidence and courage to do the right thing in any given situation.

These questions are designed to assess how you use your common sense to approach problems. There is not necessarily a "right" answer (but don't think that means there isn't a wrong answer).

One thing which you should always bear in mind when approaching such a question is that the Bar Code of Conduct's "overriding objective" states that a barrister's primary duty is to the court. Your duty to your client comes second to this followed by your duties to your solicitor, chambers and then yourself. Inevitably the questions put two or more of these duties into conflict and you have to decide how to proceed. Take your time to think about the options and use your common sense. If you think your first solution could be interpreted to suggest trickery or sharp practice then come up with another answer before you say anything aloud.

Read a guide to barristers' professional ethics—these are usually provided to all BPTC students and should be available from the library in your Inn or law school.

### 6. Current affairs questions

What chambers are looking for:

- Evidence of your analytical skills.

- Proof that you can think and respond quickly and articulately.

- A demonstration of your advocacy and ability to argue a point, especially one you may not personally believe.

- Evidence that you keep up with current affairs.

The best way to prepare for current affairs questions is to follow the news throughout the year. You should aim to read one quality newspaper daily or a weekly or internet equivalent. Read the actual "news" section, but don't ignore the editorial. This is written advocacy—and some of it is excellent. Try arguing against whatever is the proposition in issue. This is long-term preparation and will make a big difference to your knowledge-base and analysis when you get into interview. Obviously, if anything has a legal edge, pay it particular attention.

If you haven't picked up a newspaper in years, there is still a great deal you can do to prepare yourself. Before your interview you should try to do some "short-term" preparation. Sit down with a blank piece of paper and list the topics which have been making the headlines repeatedly. Again—focus particularly on the legal stories. If you can't even think of headlines, browse some of the broadsheets' websites (especially the legal sections), have a look at BBC News Online, browse back issues of The Economist or talk with a well-informed friend. It is also a good idea to look up the subject of the One Essex Court Times Law Awards essay as this will often give you at least one good legal lead.

When you have your list, decide which side of the argument you prefer and consider the reasons supporting your position. Now practise aloud spending one or two minutes putting those views forward in a persuasive way. As with debating, three is the magic number for these purposes. Try to think of three arguments supporting your case. Start your answer by highlighting your points, then go on and make them and, finally, summarise what you've just said.

After you've done this a few times, immediately consider the opposite side of the arguments. Go through exactly the same process: find three reasons and practise presenting them orally in a persuasive manner. Especially if you have a very strong view on something, it is vital to practise the opposing view. More often than not in interviews you will be asked to argue against something in which you believe or which at first glance appears to be logical. The reason is obvious: as a practising barrister you have to be able to argue any case, even one in which you do not personally believe.

A good technique is to begin by distilling the question to "first principles", identifying the fundamental issues within the debate. For example, if you are asked about some aspect of terrorism, the first principles are likely to be national security and civil liberties. Adopting this strategy will also give you a few precious seconds to decide on your position. Strengthen your answer by giving specific examples.

> **Tip:** If you aren't sure about the answer then ask for a moment or two to think about it and compose yourself. The interview panel won't mind and it gives the impression of someone who is taking control of the situation.

Remember that the panel are testing your ability to argue a case. They will challenge your position and see whether you back down under pressure. It is nearly always a mistake to do so. If you are making sensible, well-reasoned arguments, stick to them; the interviewers want to see that you will stand up to a belligerent judge and a cunning opponent. That said, a barrister must also be able to hold a mirror up to his arguments and acknowledge if they are flawed. If, half way through your answer, you realise that it is illogical and unsupportable, cut your losses and admit that you are wrong. Explain your reasons and set out your new, improved approach.

## 7. Legal questions

What chambers are looking for:

- An understanding of the overall framework of the law.

- An ability to assess facts, identify gaps in the evidence and apply the law in order to give a logical and well-structured response to a given scenario.

- Critical analysis of case law.

- In some cases, specific knowledge of an area of law.

*A Pupil*
I remember leaving one interview to be asked by the next candidate in a trembling voice 'Did they ask you about law?'

Ironically, given that candidates are about to express a passion for the law, these are often the questions that applicants dread. In fact it is not surprising that candidates fear them: the law contains a myriad of riddles and technicalities seemingly designed to trip up the unsuspecting interviewee. It can feel as if there is infinite scope for getting it wrong.

Legal problem questions often, but not always, take the same form as the problem questions set in exams: fictional scenarios with several different legal issues to identify, discuss and then resolve as best as possible. Sometimes there may be a case or a contract which you are required to read before going into the interview room.

> **Tip:** If you are given a document to read just before a pupillage interview, skim through it before diving in. If it is a judgment, you may find that the first decision is dissenting; if it is a contract, the crucial clause may be on the last page.
>
> If you are given a case to read, ensure that you have it clear in your mind what is the ratio of each judge's decision before you walk into the interview. This is an obvious opening question.

A legal question assesses two things; keep these in mind and suddenly it all seems considerably less daunting. First, a knowledge of basic legal principles. The level of knowledge of legal principles which is expected will vary considerably between different candidates and different sets. For example, if you have a PhD in a particular area of the law of trusts and are going into a chancery chambers, a deeper knowledge of equity will be expected of you than of someone currently doing the GDL in an interview at a general common law set.

Do not worry about memorising vast amounts of case law; interviewers are not looking for you to spout off every case you can think of (although they may be impressed if you can mention a couple of particularly pertinent cases). They are interested to see if you can apply principles of law to a set of facts.

> Legal problems are not designed to test detailed legal knowledge but to test essential legal common sense and essential approach to legal analysis.
> *John Furber QC, Wilberforce Chambers*

The second thing that is being assessed is an ability to think critically, to analyse the facts and law and to present a case fluently. Most chambers see this element as far more important than demonstrating actual legal knowledge. This ability to analyse and logically present your answer cannot be found in a book. You could be a brilliant lawyer with just a little legal knowledge and excellent research skills as long as you had the ability to think clearly and articulate an effective answer. Take comfort from the fact that you are using exactly the same skills that you have been taught on the GDL or law degree.

Depending on the chambers, legal problems may be sent to you days in advance or handed to you when you arrive at the interview. If you have any length of time, use it well.

If you can visit a law library between being given the problem and the interview, do so. If you are only given some time in a holding room, make notes and write down key words to remind yourself of everything you want to say, in the order that you want to say it. If there is time, run through in your head (or out loud if you are alone) exactly how you are going to express yourself.

The best way to prepare for a legal problem is to revise as if you were about to take an exam. If you have done your earlier preparation properly, you will know the chambers' practice and so may be able to predict the field of law in which you may be questioned.

Part of succeeding in interviews is talking like a barrister. This does not mean using legalese or quoting lots of cases but simply offering practical, logical solutions to any problems you are given. Read a book about procedure before your interview to help you get into this mindset.

*Richard Mott, One Essex Court*

The best form of revision for legal questions is simply to shut yourself away and read a textbook on the subject. If time is of the essence, read a revision guide. You could use your own revision notes but remember that, unlike in exams, you will rarely have a choice of questions in an interview. You will be expected to answer the question you are asked—not pick and choose which questions you like. Beware of areas you did not revise for exams as they may come up at interview.

It is worth mentioning that the area of law you need to revise might not be an area of law that you have studied. If you think that this is the case, for example with a family or employment chambers, it is even more crucial to spend a few days in the library reading a textbook (and not just a study guide) in the field. This work is an investment that should pay dividends. Imagine the interview from the interviewer's point of view. They set a problem question in, say, family law. A GDL student comes in and explains that while he is really interested in family law and cannot wait to do a family pupillage, he has never studied the area and is not even able to take a shot at the question. Another GDL student enters who has never studied family law either but he attempts the question showing a strong grasp of the key principles and proving that his interest in family is genuine. Who do you think will get the pupillage?

Another thing to consider when preparing for a legal question is to try to make sure that your law is up to date. It won't make a great impression on the interviewer if you draw a winning analogy with another case only to find that the case you have used was overturned the week before. Often legal questions are drawn up only a matter of days before the interview so they may be based on a judgment handed down very recently. Regularly read the legal press and you should not be caught out.

Legal problems are not the only form of legal questions to come up. You may be asked to give your opinion on a case (which will usually be explained) or on an aspect of law. More commonly, however, you will be asked the standard question "Which law or case would you like to change?". Make sure that you give this question some thought before going to any interview. It might be sensible to prepare a case in the field of law in which chambers specialises. Read the case that you are planning to discuss and, where relevant, read any subsequent cases which follow or distinguish that case. Online search engines and case digests can show you where each case has been cited. If you have mooted, this experience will give you an excellent source of controversial cases to discuss.

One last word of advice when tackling any legal problem: be logical. The main thing that every chambers wants to see is how your mind works. They want to see that you can break a problem down into its component parts and reassemble an insightful answer. If your thinking and logic are sound, it may not even matter if you get the conclusion slightly wrong.

*Any Questions?*

At the end of an interview you may be asked by the panel if you have any questions for them. On its face this is simply a chance to clarify any queries you may have about pupillage, practice or chambers—but remember, you are still being assessed. With this question you have a final opportunity to impress the panel with an insightful question that demonstrates your commitment to that chambers or to some element of their practice. However, if you ask a weak question, you may leave the interview on a low note. If in doubt, heed the words attributed to Abraham Lincoln: "Better to remain silent and be thought a fool, than to speak and remove all doubt".

## Mock Interviews

Practice interviews are invaluable. Seize all opportunities to do them.
                                                    *Jennie Gillies, 4 Pump Court*

It is likely that your local careers service will offer some form of mock interview. Even if this is not specifically for pupillage, it is an excellent chance to be asked unexpected questions and to be given unbiased feedback about how you appear to a stranger. You can give brilliant answers but if you slouch in your chair, start every answer with "like" or fiddle with your watch, you will not be invited back. You need to appear confident and calm, make eye contact and give clear answers. Any form of mock interview will help you work towards this.

If there are no mock interviews on offer at your law school or careers service, ask a friend if they can give you one and request that they give you constructive feedback. Even better, if you have a friendly sponsor in your Inn they might be willing to give you some help and advice (but think twice before asking them if you are applying to their chambers).

Ask them to give you honest—and blunt—feedback about what you are doing, whether right or wrong. The career you are trying to get into is not one well-suited to sensitivities. Do not take it personally if someone criticises something about your words or your manner. Ask if you kept eye contact, if you sounded passionate, if you were fidgeting or have any distracting habits, and if there were any other weaknesses. Find out the problem areas on which you need to concentrate. Listen to all advice that is given: learn, evaluate and change.

Whether or not you are able to have a mock interview, spend some time on the day before your interview running through answers to questions that you think are likely to come up. Practise your answers aloud in front of a mirror and iron out any areas where you feel unsure.

## Before the Interview

*Know Where to Go*

Make sure you know exactly where chambers is located, and how to get there, prior to leaving for the interview.

> **How to Enter the Inns at Weekends:** Many interviews take place at weekends. During weekends, the normal entrances to the Inns of Court will be locked and you will only be able to enter through certain access points. Make sure that you know how to get into chambers so that you do not spend valuable time running around the perimeters of an Inn making you flustered or late.
>
> - Lincoln's Inn—Lincoln's Inn Fields entrance.
>
> - Middle and Inner Temple—Tudor Street entrance.
>
> - Gray's Inn—Gray's Inn Road entrance.

It might be advisable to locate the relevant chambers the weekend before your interview and check that you know where the entrance can be found.

*Last Minute Preparation*

The night or morning before the interview, read through all the notes that you have compiled on the chambers so that they are fresh in your head—particularly the areas of law in which the chambers specialises and the reasons why you want to go there.

### On the Day Do's and Don'ts

Do:

- Make sure that you have two shirts freshly ironed just in case you get toothpaste down one.

- Make sure that your shoes are polished.

- Make sure that your suit looks smart.

- Ladies—if you are wearing tights (and if you are wearing a skirt you should be, whatever the weather!), take a spare pair with you—it is uncanny how ladders appear when an interview is imminent.

- Gentlemen—if you normally shave, remember to do so.

- Turn off your mobile phone the moment you arrive at chambers (though not before in case chambers needs to reach you at the last minute).

Don't:

- Wear overpowering scent or aftershave.

*In the Waiting Room*

Your behaviour might be watched from the moment you set foot inside chambers. Make sure that you behave accordingly. Be friendly towards anyone you come into contact with, be they receptionists, clerks or pupils—they may be asked for their opinion later by the panel and they may even be undercover barristers from that chambers.

If you are sitting in a waiting room, do not listen to your iPod and do not chat on your mobile phone.

Check your appearance before you go in to the interview. Better to find out before the interview that you have ink on your face or your shirt collar is at a jaunty angle.

**The Last Word**

The Bar rewards persistence.

*Maya Lester, Brick Court Chambers*

If you are not offered pupillage the first time round, keep trying. Many candidates who eventually get pupillage only do so having applied several times. Unlike in many other professions, your second application is not damaged by the fact that you have tried once before; indeed, it can demonstrate your determination. Get as much legal experience as you can and further prove your resolve.

Do not despair if you are unsuccessful in obtaining a pupillage first time round. Make the extra year work to your advantage, both in terms of the additional relevant experience that you will be able to acquire, further to enhance your CV, and in terms of the additional maturity that you will be able to bring to the process the following year. Few (if any) chambers operate a bar on candidates re-applying. Do however consider whether you made the correct choice of chambers first time round.

*Colin Wynter QC, Devereux Chambers*

Good luck!

# 23 PICKING YOUR PUPILLAGE

With most applicants unsuccessful in their search for pupillage, it may seem somewhat optimistic to write a chapter about how to choose which pupillage to accept. Nonetheless, each year there are a select and lucky few who are offered more than one. If you find yourself among this crème de la crème, here are some of the points you might wish to consider.

## How to Approach Your Choice

Choosing a pupillage might be one of the biggest decisions you will ever make. It will shape your future areas of specialism, your future income and your future practice. You could go on to become a leading expert in one of chambers' practice areas which you had not previously considered. Members of chambers may become some of your closest friends. Chambers may prosper and expand, or sink into the red and disband. Moreover, with ongoing disputes over legal aid funding, the forthcoming deregulation of legal services and the increase in solicitor-advocates, the Bar faces many challenges in the coming years; you will want to be in a chambers ready to deal with the trials ahead.

Inevitably, during the application process you will find that an order of preference emerges in your mind. It is however common to find that during the interview process your perceptions change entirely. Those chambers that looked excellent on paper may not have impressed you with their interview process, while your reserve choice may have made an excellent impression. You will usually have just two weeks in which to accept an offer of pupillage so it is worth giving some consideration to the decision before the date on which offers are made.

> **Tip:** If you have a string of questions or want to ask about the more delicate issues such as your future earnings, wait until you have the pupillage offer in your hand. Although you should not be afraid to ask questions, once you have the offer, chambers should really be trying to woo you—ask probing questions too early and you may look overconfident and jeopardise your chances.

*A Pupil:*

I knew which chambers I wanted to go to when I was filling out my application form—at least I thought I did. That was until I met the visibly bored interview panel whose lacklustre questions and demeanour barely concealed their distain for me and the other applicants. It made me think 'If they can't be bothered to interview me properly, will they bother to train me properly?'. Although I was fortunate enough to be offered the pupillage, I turned it down in the end and went somewhere else.

By the time chambers has made you an offer, they have already decided that you are the best candidate: it is now their turn to impress you. In order to make your choice, you will want to have as much information as possible about each set. If you have not already done a mini-pupillage with them, ask if you can spend a day in chambers. This will give you a chance to see the nature of the work and also to meet some of the barristers and even pupil-supervisors you would be working with. Ask if you can speak to the current pupil or a junior tenant to talk about their experiences. This is your opportunity to ask *them* questions: take advantage of it.

Choose your set with care. I do not subscribe to the view that any old pupillage will do. That set may not even be there in 12 months' time. Take advice about which are the good, solid, well respected sets and go there. Otherwise, if you aren't taken on, you may really struggle to get third sixes or tenancy elsewhere.

*Eleanor Searley, 6 King's Bench Walk*

**Factors to Consider**

There are a number of things to weigh up when you find yourself deciding between more than one offer.

*Prospects of Tenancy*

Throughout law school, pupillage itself seems like the holy grail. Yet as soon as you begin your first six, you will find that the goalposts have once again shifted and tenancy is your new aim. If you are in the lucky position of having more than one pupillage in hand, start thinking about your prospects of being taken on at each of the sets.

There are some chambers which offer pupillage "with a view to tenancy". They take as many pupils as there are future tenancies in chambers and they consider pupils an investment. If the pupils live up to their potential, they will comfortably sail into tenancy. Other sets routinely take on more pupils than there are possible places for tenants.

*A Former Pupil:*
I went to a prestigious chambers where there is always a large number of pupils. I didn't really realise the implications of this in terms of the unhealthy competitiveness that grew between us as a result of the fact that we were all after just one spot. Perhaps I am bitter but looking back it was a great wheeze for chambers—we were cheap, highly-trained labour who worked every waking hour doing all the poorly paid low-end work, each pretending that we were loving every moment. It was miserable. Needless to say, they didn't take me on.

Before you make your choice, look at how many pupillages are being offered and how many tenancies there might be at the end. You should be able to deduce this information from the pupillage guides or chambers' websites but if not, ask. Look at chambers' track record for recruitment and check to see whether they regularly take on their own pupils or prefer to recruit third six pupils. Ask whether the current pupils have been taken on.

**A word of consolation:** Remember that recruitment can go in waves—one year all four pupils may be offered tenancy and the following year, no offers will be made. Do not be too disheartened if you learn that your chambers has just rejected all their pupils shortly before you start—this may give you better prospects of success.

You may also want to give more consideration to those sets where you are their first choice as opposed to those offers that you have been made off the back of a reserve list. Members of chambers will know whether you were their first choice and this may play a part in the sort of first impression you are able to make. If you are one of two but you know that your co-pupil was their first choice and you were a reserve, you may be starting at a small disadvantage. This is not something which is likely to make a huge difference in the long run but in chambers where there is significant competition for tenancy, it may be something you wish to consider.

*The Pupillage Award and Future Earnings*

Pupillage awards vary dramatically from as little as £10,000 plus earnings at a criminal chambers up to £60,000 plus earnings for 12 months at a top commercial set. Although in reality few students will be choosing between such extremes, you may find yourself faced with a significant disparity in remuneration.

*A Pupil:*
There was £10,000 difference in the guaranteed earnings between the two sets where I was offered pupillages. It made it a very tough choice because I was inclined towards the less affluent chambers but had a mountain of student debt behind me. In the end I took a long-term view and opted for the lower award at the set where I thought I would be happier. It was definitely the right decision for me and I haven't looked back.

*A Junior Tenant:*
The large awards in their tens of thousands can be extremely alluring, particularly after years of student poverty. There needs to be a degree of caution, however, in using that headline figure as your guide to which set of chambers to pick. Some chambers use a large award to entice pupils who might ordinarily be attracted to more prestigious sets. Yet the sum of money offered may not reflect the calibre of the set, or your future earning potential there. Some civil and general common law sets offer awards comparable with those of large commercial sets, but the potential future rewards can be markedly different.

If one of your options is a chambers which specialises in publicly-funded work (i.e. crime, family or human rights work), you will also need to think about the serious impact that doing this work will have on your bank balance. The sad reality is that earnings at the junior end are very low—and low by any standards, not simply when compared to those of other barristers. Do not be afraid to ask what junior tenants are actually *earning* and not just billing: payment can be extremely slow and sometimes fail to materialise altogether.

*A Junior Tenant:*
If you are desperate to do only publicly-funded work give serious consideration to whether you can afford it. Work out the minimum you need to earn per month and ask pupils currently at the Bar if that is a regular amount for them to earn.

*Practice*

There are a number of different aspects to consider when looking at your potential practice. Obviously you need to consider the practice areas—not just which area of law do you want to practise but does one of the chambers do more of this sort of work?

Think about the lifestyle implications of each practice area. A general common law practice may involve being in court every day, receiving the brief the night before and leading a more spontaneous existence. A shipping practice could involve regular hours, lots of paperwork and almost no advocacy for the first few years. Ask junior members of chambers what their practices are really like: do they spend a great deal of time travelling? Are they busy? Do they share rooms or work alone? Who do they ask for advice? Which aspects of their practices do they most enjoy? What would they change? Also consider whether you want to practise in a range of fields or would prefer to specialise early and look at which chambers offer these opportunities.

*Atmosphere*

Arguably the most important of all the factors to consider is whether you think you will feel at home in your chambers. If you find somewhere where you feel you belong, you are far more likely to thrive; if you get on with the members of chambers, you will have a greater prospect of being taken on. This is a matter entirely for your own judgment. While you may want to think about such aspects as whether you want to be in a large or small chambers, what this really comes down to is one question—ask yourself "will I be happy here?".

*A Junior Tenant:*
I was lucky enough to find myself with a number of offers. The one I accepted was not the most prestigious, the best paid or the most

glamorous—it was just the one where I felt most at home and thought I would be happy. My friends told me that I had made the wrong choice but if I had gone to the top set, I would have felt overwhelmed and out of my depth. As it was, I had found a set where I felt there were like-minded people who would help me to grow as a barrister. I was taken on at the end of my pupillage and I know that I made the right decision.

# 24 THIRD SIXES

The term "third six" refers to a third six months of pupillage following the first and second six which make up the traditional 12 months of pupillage. A third six allows those pupils who have not been offered tenancy after pupillage to undergo a further period of pupillage either at the chambers where they did pupillage or, more commonly, elsewhere. This allows the pupil a further chance to demonstrate his abilities to a chambers, usually with a view to being offered tenancy at the end.

## Handling Rejection and Moving Forwards

First of all, remember that a great many successful barristers, including successful silks, were turned down following their first pupillage. Rejection from tenancy remains common across the Bar. The simple fact that the chambers where you did pupillage has decided not to offer you a tenancy does not mean that another chambers will feel the same. There are a myriad of reasons why pupils are not taken on and there should be no stigma attached to those who find themselves in this position.

Almost inevitably, not being offered tenancy will bring bitter disappointment. You will have worked extremely hard and may feel you have built up positive relationships with many members of Chambers, solicitors and clerks. It is all too easy to take the rejection personally and to let it affect those relationships you have worked to develop. Resist this temptation. Be gracious and learn from the feedback you are given. Members of chambers can be crucial in helping in your hunt for a third six and some of your solicitors may even give you work at your new chambers. If you are able to say that you have loyal solicitors and can bring work with you, you will make yourself a much more attractive applicant. The worst thing you can do is to let your relationship with your chambers break down.

Before you embark upon third six applications, it is worth spending some time thinking about where you went wrong. You may want to ask yourself whether this is the right area of law for you. Have you enjoyed the work you have done as a pupil? Have you enjoyed being in court? Have you enjoyed the lifestyle of a barrister? While rejection from tenancy is by no means an indication that you are not cut out for a career at the Bar, it does give you an opportunity to reassess your career and think about whether you really want to be a barrister.

*A former third six pupil:*
Do not be frightened by third sixes, they can be the best thing that happen to you. We all have to find our fit and it may not happen the first time—you will soon discover there are many tenants in chambers who started out their lives as pupils at other sets, who will have tales of woe that make your previous 12 months seem like a delight. You will be judged on how good you are, not on the basis you are a third six pupil. And don't forget, you have a whole 12 months' advantage in experience and knowledge over the fresh-faced first six pupils who are still struggling to come to terms with their alarm clocks going off before midday.

If things do not work out at your first chambers it can sometimes be a blessing in disguise. I started out at a civil and commercial set of chambers. The people were lovely and supportive, but the work was not for me. It was miserable, no matter how charming my pupil supervisors were. I moved across to crime at the end of my 12 months and found myself in a set of chambers where I instantly felt more at home. My third six went well; I loved the work this time, and I think it showed. I am now coming to the end of 12 months as a tenant and could not be happier.

**Third Six Applications**

In the vast majority of cases, applications are made by CV and covering letter. The advice in Chapter 21 applies equally to third six applications.

*Choosing where to Apply*

Unlike 12 month pupillages, there is no central and comprehensive source that lists third six pupillages. Many will be advertised on the Bar Council website (see address in the Resources section at the back of the book) but this is rarely an exhaustive list. A large number of sets will only advertise vacancies on their own website. Additionally, speculative applications can be fruitful: even though a set is not advertising for a third six pupil, it may consider outstanding applications.

The best advice is to speak to as many people as you can and research carefully online. Ask your friends and members of chambers which sets are recruiting. Many pupils find that pupil-supervisors speak to members of different sets in order to try to find a space. If you have developed a good working relationship with your clerks during pupillage, consider asking them if they know of any vacancies.

*A former third six pupil:*
Members of Chambers usually enjoy helping former pupils find third sixes. Many take pride in it and see it as part of their role. Be aware of this: do not burn bridges if you are told that you have been unsuccessful in your tenancy application.

If you turned down pupillage at other sets these places should be your first ports of call. Politely remind them that you were offered pupillage with them and that you would like to apply for a third six if they have a vacancy.

The CV of a prospective third six pupil should include clear examples of the work done in the first and second six. Be sure to tailor experiences to the expertise of the set to which you are applying: blanket applications are wholly unimpressive.

*A former third six pupil:*
Bear in mind that many potential recruiters will approach third sixers with an attitude of 'if they weren't good enough for XYZ Chambers why should they be good enough for this set?'. This is a question that should be dealt with, ideally by your referees from the set at which you did pupillage. You are unlikely to be asked the question directly, but you need to have thought carefully about your answer just in case. Speak to as many people as possible who have taken the third six route.

When you are considering where to apply for a third six, be aware that you may have to compromise or be flexible in terms of location, area of law or quality of set. That said, do not be afraid to cast your net wide. Whilst it would be unusual for one set to take as a third six pupil an individual who had spent 12 months at a less prestigious set, this does occasionally happen.

*Successful Applications*

There are two important ways to strengthen your chances as a third six applicant, above and beyond those set out in Chapter 21 above. The first is to make your application early. The market for third six pupils is most active between June and August each year: it is during these months that the majority of pupils receive their tenancy decisions. Be aware that sets that are looking to recruit a third six pupil will make offers as soon as they have found a candidate that they like. This can mean that even over the course of a few weeks in July/early August most of the third six positions will be filled. Unlike first six pupillages, there are as yet no Bar Council rules governing the timing of third six applications and offers. It is therefore extremely advantageous to make your applications as early as possible

To a large extent you are of course bound by the date of the tenancy decision in your set. There is little you can do to control this. However, in order to mitigate the effect of a late tenancy decision you can do two things in advance of the decision. First, make sure that you have given thought to where you will apply if you are not taken on. Secondly, ensure that your applications are ready to be printed and sent off. This will save you precious days if the decision goes against you.

In most cases, it would not be sensible to apply for third sixes before you have received your tenancy decision. The obvious exceptions to this are if you have been given a very clear indication by your first set that you have poor prospects or in the unusual situation where you have decided that even if you were offered tenancy you would reject it. Until you have been given your decision, your focus should be on securing tenancy at the set at which you are currently a pupil. Whilst some tenants in your set may think it entirely sensible to "cover your back" by investigating third six options, many may think it shows a lack of commitment. Word travels quickly at the Bar and tenants at your original set may doubt your commitment if they hear that you are applying elsewhere.

The second thing you can do is get a strong reference from the set at which you did pupillage. You should be sure to include as a referee a barrister at the set that has first-hand experience of your work. It will often be a pupil-supervisor or the head of the pupillage committee, or perhaps both. The questions that all recruiters will be looking to have answered are "why was this applicant not taken on?" and "why would they do well in our set?".

*A former third six pupil:*
If you have been rejected, start your applications straight away. Be systematic and don't rule anything out without good reason. Make as many applications as possible. Put time into each application so it is personal to the chambers in question. Accept that this is going to be a lot of work and get on with it immediately. Seek the advice of as many barristers as possible, including the barristers at your current set. This flatters them, makes you look keen and humble, and might persuade them to put in some calls to help you out.

Be courteous to people at the set which has rejected you. Take the rejection graciously, even if you feel unfairly treated.

*Fourth Sixes*

It is possible to do any number of third sixes (fourth sixes, fifth sixes . . .). Large chambers who are keen for third six pupils to see as many members of chambers as possible frequently ask pupils to stay on after a third six in order to ensure that pupils have had adequate exposure before a tenancy decision. There is however a risk that pupils are being exploited by being kept in limbo without a tenancy. At the time of writing, the issue was being investigated by a Bar Standards Board Working Group.

*Squatting*

Finally, a word about "squatting". This is a temporary measure whereby a set will allow someone (usually a former pupil) to remain in Chambers but not as a tenant nor as a pupil. You will be given work by the clerks but usually only the work which no one in chambers is able to cover. The purpose is to enable you to support yourself while you apply for a third six elsewhere. Squatting is relatively unusual and is entirely at each individual set's discretion.

# 25 A POST SCRIPT FROM LORD NEUBERGER OF ABBOTSBURY

I would like to add a word about widening access to the Bar, because it is so important and because it was the remit of the working party I chaired. As far as possible, access to the Bar (and indeed maintaining a career at the Bar) must be, and must be seen to be, equally achievable by all, irrespective of gender, age, ethnicity, religion, sexual orientation, physical ability, financial circumstances, social status, or educational advantage. That should be true of any career, but it is particularly important for the Bar. First, the Bar is a high profile profession which prides itself on its excellence; it should therefore be, and be seen to be, in the vanguard of progress, and it should ensure that it really attracts the best people, which means fishing in as big a pool as possible. Secondly, a barrister advises and speaks for all types of people in what for them are very important circumstances; accordingly, within limits (bearing in mind the qualities needed for practice), the Bar, at all levels, should be representative of Society. Thirdly, it is from the ranks of the senior Bar that the majority of judges are selected, and public confidence in the judiciary is in danger of being undermined if the judges are seen as a group as being too male, too white, too public school, and too much from advantaged backgrounds.

In very brief terms, a more balanced profile for the Bar, or indeed for the judiciary, should not be achieved by positive discrimination, if that means selecting by reference to criteria other than merit. I suggest that there should be a three-pronged initiative to recruit more people with the requisite suitable qualities who come from the relatively under-represented groups. First, they should be encouraged to consider the Bar as a career; secondly, assistance should be available to enable them to embark on such a career; thirdly we should enable them to maintain a career at the Bar. The encouragement involves information and meetings; the assistance requires funding and more open-mindedness; the enabling means facilitating a change of attitude where necessary within the legal profession: barristers, clerks, clients, solicitors, and law schools. One cannot expect a single profession, least of all one as numerically small as the Bar, to cure, or even wholly to compensate for the inequalities of Society, but that is no excuse for not trying to reduce their effect. There is quite a long way to go, but we are at least travelling in the right direction.

For more information on the Entry to the Bar Working Party's Report please visit *www.barcouncil.org.uk/consultations/Reports*.

# APPENDICES

# 26 FUNDING

Qualifying as a barrister is expensive. Fees for the BPTC alone currently range from about £8,500 to over £14,500. Add a law degree or GDL and living expenses and you quickly see how significant an investment it constitutes.

Beyond Inns scholarships (see Chapter 5), there are several ways of funding your training.

## Law School Scholarships

Some law schools offer scholarships. These take the form of a partial or complete waiver in fees rather than a cash hand-out. Applications are made by way of standard application forms or essay competitions, usually before the course begins. Contact your provider for further details.

## Chambers Awards

For those lucky few who get pupillage before the BPTC, some chambers will make grants to their future pupils who are about to undertake the BPTC. This is known as "drawing down" your pupillage award. Beware that anything you are given will usually be deducted from the award you receive during pupillage. If you have pupillage, contact your set to find out more.

## Career Development Loans

These specialist bank loans are good value during the course but interest payments start immediately after. This could be a problem if you haven't secured pupillage before beginning the BPTC.

## Bank Overdraft

Some banks allow students an interest-free overdraft facility but this will only cover a relatively small part of the BPTC costs.

**Bank Loans**

For most students a bank loan is inevitable. This is without doubt the most expensive of the options for funding the BPTC; be sure to research loans very carefully. Some banks are now offering relatively favourable rates of interest for loans which are specifically to fund the BPTC. Initiatives providing these "soft loans" are becoming increasingly common.

**Discretionary Local Educational Authority (LEA) Awards**

Some LEAs offer awards for people about to begin professional courses. This is worth investigation, but you should be aware that there are very few such awards, and even fewer made for the BPTC.

**Part-Time Study**

It is possible to do the law degree, the GDL and the BPTC part-time. This can be a useful option if you are in full-time employment, struggling financially or have family commitments.

**Delay Study**

Some people choose to work for a few years after the academic stage of training and before starting the BPTC. For many people this means working as a paralegal, enabling them to gain legal experience at the same time as saving money to pay for their training. Look at the suggestions in Chapters 15 and 20 for ideas for work which will be relevant to your practice area.

# 27 SOLICITORS CONVERTING TO THE BAR

The ability to manage several cases at the same time, handle clients sensitively and apply the law to practical problems are just some of the skills that a practising solicitor can bring to a career at the Bar. Whether it is through a sense of frustration in handing over cases to a barrister for trial, a desire for the greater flexibility that being self-employed allows, or simply a craving for change, it is becoming increasingly common for solicitors to convert to the Bar. Despite this, finding out about the process can be challenging.

## Making the Change

As a solicitor there are essentially two hurdles to overcome before you can begin practising as a self-employed barrister. First, you must satisfy the Bar Standards Board's requirements so that you may hold yourself out as a practising barrister. Secondly, you must obtain tenancy. Although related, the two are distinct challenges.

### The BSB Rules

The rules governing the conversion process are set out in detail in the *Bar Training Regulations* at Regulation 59. This document is available on the BSB's website and requires careful reading. The following is a simplified summary.

The process of transferring is governed by the Qualifications Committee of the Bar Standards Board. All solicitors must first apply to the Qualifications Committee and pay an administration fee, which at the time of writing is £400. The application is a standard form available from the BSB website. You must set out in detail your qualification and experience as a solicitor, including any rights of audience you have earned. Included with the application should be a certificate of good standing issued by the Law Society and a declaration that you are a fit and proper person to be called to the Bar.

It is necessary also for all solicitors to complete six qualifying sessions (see Chapter 5), or undertake that you will do so within three years of Call.

Beyond these two requirements, the rules are designed to take into account differences in applicants' levels and types of experience. Compare the experience of a solicitor with higher rights of audience in both civil and criminal courts, who has been acting as an advocate in the courts for ten years, with another solicitor who has been an associate at a magic circle firm for just one year and has never been to court. The rules allow flexibility to take these factors into account.

Solicitors without higher rights of audience will be required to take (i) an aptitude test and (ii) pupillage, or part thereof. There are two parts to the aptitude test: advocacy and ethics. Both are oral examinations. The Qualifications Committee will determine, based on the information contained in your written application, whether you are required to pass either or both. Usually it is only those solicitors with no significant advocacy experience who are required to pass the advocacy section. In addition, you will almost always be required to undertake at least some period of practising pupillage, according to your experience. The following guidelines are provided by the Qualifications Committee:

a. A newly-qualified solicitor will usually be required to undertake six months of non-practising pupillage and six months of practising pupillage.

b. A solicitor of less than five years' experience will usually be required to undertake three to six months of non-practising pupillage and six months of practising pupillage.

c. A solicitor of more than five years' experience may be exempted from the whole of the non-practising period of pupillage or required to undertake up to three months of such period and will usually also be required to undertake three to six months of practising pupillage.

In determining the precise period of pupillage to be required the Qualifications Committee will take into account the nature and extent of the solicitor's experience, particularly significant advocacy experience. You would therefore be well-advised to make your experience clear on your written application.

For a solicitor with higher rights of audience in either civil or criminal proceedings (but not both) the rules are different. In this instance, you will be exempt from all parts of the aptitude test and will ordinarily be exempt from the usual pupillage requirements. It is only in exceptional circumstances, taking into account such factors as experience, previous practice and intended future practice, that you may be required to undertake a period of pupillage.

A solicitor with higher rights of audience in both civil and criminal proceedings will be exempt from all parts of the aptitude test and from all pupillage requirements. In effect, the Qualifications Committee will allow you to act as a practising barrister without any further professional training or experience.

*Tenancy*

Whether or not you are required by the BSB to undertake a period of pupillage, you may find in practical terms that this is essential in order to secure tenancy. For obvious reasons, almost all sets will be highly reticent about offering a tenancy to someone based solely on an interview. Moreover, being a barrister requires a very different skill-set from being a solicitor and it can be difficult to make the leap without some practical experience. Pupillage can serve as a valuable transitional stage for you, as well as giving chambers the opportunity to decide whether you are of sufficient calibre to be offered a permanent place in chambers. For both these reasons, you should be prepared, whatever your status, to spend at least six months doing pupillage. This, in turn, means that you must be ready to face the extreme competition of pupillage applications.

Be aware that many chambers may be unclear about the rules for solicitors transferring to the Bar. Some may even assume that you are automatically required to do 12 months' pupillage, in the same way as other applicants. It is therefore sensible to make contact with sets before you apply. Enquire as to whether they have a particular policy and whether they would expect to receive your application through the Pupillage Portal or by CV and covering letter. Do not leave this to the last minute.

Play to your strengths in your application. Whatever your current area of practice as a solicitor you should have relevant experience on which you can draw. Most solicitors who convert to become barristers, but by no means all, move from their firm's litigation department. One of your key selling points in this situation will be your experience handling lay clients and managing a case. Take advantage of this. You may also be able to bring contacts to chambers and thereby bring in work.

Previous experience as a solicitor gives you a great insight into what solicitors want from the Bar and into what it's like to give difficult advice to a lay client. I know what it's like from the solicitor's point of view to deal with good counsel and that is what I try to emulate.

*Robert Purves, 3 Verulam Buildings*

As a solicitor, you will have seen how a case develops from cradle to grave and become familiar with the nuts and bolts of litigation. You are also likely to have had significant exposure to lay clients and will therefore be aware of their strategic objectives in the litigation process and what they expect from their lawyers. You will also be acutely aware of the demands of the solicitor's job. That accumulated knowledge and experience should smooth your transition to the Bar, make pupillage less daunting and enable you to focus on developing your oral and written advocacy skills.

*Damien Walker, Essex Court Chambers*

It is also important, however, to make it clear that you will be approaching the job with a "willing to learn" attitude. Whatever your experience and ability, as a pupil you will be expected to work hard, sometimes on relatively mundane tasks. You should satisfy the barristers that interview you that you do not consider yourself too grand to do whatever is required of you.

### Planning ahead:
If done properly, applying for pupillage is an extremely time-consuming process. You should start your research and your applications far in advance of any deadlines.

Think about which chambers you wish to apply to and research them thoroughly. You may already have the advantage of having built up relationships with barristers in those sets and may therefore be able to ask them about their experience of chambers and whether they are recruiting.

The pupillage application process will involve attending interviews and perhaps mini-pupillages, too. These can cause problems for someone with a full-time job, particularly given the sensitivities of applying for a different career.

Communicate with the sets to which you are applying. If you face particular problems, the set may be able to accommodate them. However, be careful to show that you are committed. Interviews and assessed mini-pupillages are a drain on the time of practising barristers as well as the candidates. Be aware of this.

Interviews and mini-pupillages can consume several days. Be sure to plan your holiday in advance to ensure that you have enough left to take the necessary time off. Resist the temptation to disregard the sets that seemingly demand more of your time: spending time within chambers gives you a valuable impression of the differences between sets.

## Practical Considerations

*Timing*

The structure of law firms is such that it is generally—although not universally—the case that, as you become more senior, you will spend an increasing percentage of your time managing others, performing administrative tasks and engaging in business development. A move to the Bar will enable you to spend the vast majority of your time on legal research, analytical work, drafting and, of course, advocacy.

*Damien Walker, Essex Court Chambers*

One common point that is often of concern is whether there is a "right time" to convert. The reality is that people successfully make the transition at all stages of their careers. There are however a few factors to consider. First, be aware that the more senior you become as a solicitor the greater will be the drop in income when you start at the Bar. You must be prepared for this. Secondly, chambers may be more impressed if you can demonstrate that you have shown some flair as a solicitor. This may involve running your own cases and/or liaising directly with clients. Depending on your area of expertise and the firm in which you worked it may take several years to develop this experience. Finally, many solicitors find that as they become more senior their work begins to involve less law and more management and business development. This can be unattractive to some, as well as being further removed from the work of a barrister.

> The higher you go up in a big organisation the more limited the opportunities to advance and to apply your expertise in new areas—the Bar offered me a good opportunity to be my own boss.
>
> *Robert Purves, 3 Verulam Buildings*

### Burning Bridges

Be sensitive in your handling of the transition. If you do not anticipate having the support of your superiors, consider who you will use as a professional referee. In any event, do not burn any bridges: the contacts you have developed in your firm of solicitors can be a source of work when you begin practice.

### Other Considerations

Building a career in any profession takes time and effort: think carefully and do as much research as possible before making a commitment to change. Two points in particular are often given insufficient weight.

First, do not underestimate the competition. Your success as a solicitor is not necessarily a measure of your potential as a barrister. Chambers will be looking for clear evidence that you are going to be, or are already, an outstanding advocate. A successful solicitor's practice does not necessarily prove this. Secondly, consider the social aspect—being a barrister can be significantly more lonely. Whereas in a firm of solicitors you may be accustomed to secretarial staff, trainees, associates and partners, in chambers barristers tend to work on their own cases more often than in large teams.

**Factors to consider:**
If you are interested in transferring the Bar, there are a number of points which you may wish to consider. No matter how hard you worked as a solicitor, you will find yourself working harder at the Bar. This seems to be the experience of those who have made the transition successfully. Second, it is crucial to plan ahead and talk to prospective chambers in good time to secure pupillage. Tenancy is never a given and you need to think carefully about where you may want to be in practice. Third, you

should never burn your bridges with old colleagues. The Bar does not work out for all prospective transferees for a variety of reasons and you may need to return to practice as a solicitor. In my own experience, I have been the privileged recipient of instructions from many people whom I first encountered as solicitors or worked with over the years. My early years in practice were founded in part upon the loyalty of those solicitors and for whose support I remain deeply grateful.

*Martin Palmer, Littleton Chambers*

# 28 GLOSSARY

Advocacy
: The act of persuading the judge, jury or the other side that your case is right. Advocacy can be written or oral.

Advocate
: Often used synonymously with the term "barrister", an advocate is one who argues a case.

Alternative Dispute Resolution
: Frequently referred to as "ADR", this is a way to avoid court by resolving the dispute without recourse to conventional litigation. It encompasses, among others, mediation, arbitration and negotiation.

Arbitration
: The determination of a dispute by a neutral third party rather than by a court.

Authority
: A judicial decision or other source of law used to support a proposition.

Bands
: A white necktie worn as part of traditional court attire.

The Bar
: All barristers.

Bar Council
: The governing body of the Bar.

Bar school
: A provider where you can take the BPTC.

| | |
|---|---|
| Bar Standards Board | The body regulating the Bar. |
| The bench | The judiciary. |
| Bencher | Another word for a Master of the Bench. |
| Bibling | The term used by solicitors for indexing documents. |
| Blawg | A law-related blog. |
| Brief | The documents from a solicitor setting out a barrister's instructions in a case. |
| Bundle | The documents provided to court in advance of a hearing. |
| BPTC | The Bar Practical Training Course, the final stage of training before pupillage. |
| BVC | The Bar Vocational Course, the old name for the what is now the BPTC. |
| Call | An abbreviation of call to the Bar. |
| Call to the Bar (also referred to as Call Night) | The ceremony following graduation from the BPTC. The ceremony confers on you the title of barrister. |
| Chambers | Most commonly, the name given to a group of barristers operating together to share expenses. Chambers' name is often simply its address.<br><br>In this context, "chambers" is synonymous with "set" or "set of chambers". |

| | |
|---|---|
| Chambers—*cont.* | Note that the word "chambers" is used for both the singular and plural. |
| | Another use of "chambers" refers to a judge's office. |
| Chambers' evening | An evening either in chambers or at a law school where chambers promote their pupillages to students. |
| Chancery | Work focusing primarily on property, trusts and wills. |
| Circuit | A geographical area of England and Wales with courts and barristers working within it. There are six circuits: the Midland, North Eastern, Northern, South Eastern, Wales and Chester and Western Circuits. |
| Claimant | The party that brings a claim in court. |
| Clerks | The administrative team within chambers which organises the barristers' diaries, negotiates their payment with the solicitors and ensures that fees are paid. |
| Conference or con | A meeting, usually between barrister, solicitor and the lay client. |
| Counsel | Another term for barrister, both singular and plural. |
| CPE | The Common Professional Examination, a law conversion course akin to the GDL. |

| | |
|---|---|
| Crown Prosecution Service or CPS | The body responsible for prosecuting criminal cases in England and Wales. |
| Devilling | Work done by a junior member of chambers for a more senior member; the junior member is known as a "devil". |
| Dining | Having dinner in your Inn. This is the most common form of qualifying session. |
| Door tenant | An associate of chambers rather than a full member. Door tenants tend not to have their own rooms in chambers. |
| Employed Bar | Barristers who work as employees (for example in the CPS or as in-house counsel), rather than at the self-employed Bar. |
| First six | The first six months of pupillage (during which pupils cannot take their own cases). |
| FRU | The Free Representation Unit. A charity training law students to provide free representation for those who could not otherwise afford it (primarily in social security and employment cases). |
| GDL | The one year qualifying law course taken by non-law graduates. This is the more recent version of the CPE and is often referred to as the "Law Conversion Course". |

| | |
|---|---|
| Government Legal Service or GLS | The organisation of lawyers who work as civil servants in almost all major departments of the UK Government. |
| Gray's Inn | One of the four Inns of Court. |
| Higher rights of audience | The right to appear in the Crown Courts, High Court, Court of Appeal and Supreme Court. Only gained by barristers following six months of pupillage. |
| Independent Bar | The term formerly used to describe those practising barristers who are self-employed. |
| In-house counsel | A barrister employed to work in a private company or solicitors' firm. |
| Inner Temple | One of the four Inns of Court. |
| The Inns of Court | Four historic legal societies for barristers located in central London (see Chapter 5). |
| Instructing solicitor | The solicitor who instructs the barrister (i.e. gives him the brief) for a particular case. |
| Judiciary | Judges. |
| Junior | A barrister who has not been appointed Queen's Counsel. |
| | Also the term for a less experienced barrister working on a case being led by a more senior barrister. |

| | |
|---|---|
| Jurisprudence | Technically meaning the theory and philosophy of law, this term is also used to refer to the entire body of law in a jurisdiction. |
| KC | King's Counsel. The name for a silk when a king is on the throne. |
| Knifing | A debating term referring to a team undermining their own side by fundamentally disagreeing with them. |
| Law Society | The body representing solicitors in England and Wales. |
| Lawyer | A general term referring to both barristers and solicitors. |
| Lay client | The person with a legal problem who instructs the barrister (usually through a solicitor) to assist in resolving it. |
| Leader | The most senior barrister working on a case. |
| Legalese | Legal jargon. |
| Lincoln's Inn | One of the four Inns of Court. |
| Litigant in person | A self-represented party. |
| Litigation | Contentious legal action (rather than purely advisory work). |
| LLB | The letters written after a name to indicate that person holds a Bachelor of Laws. |

| | |
|---|---|
| LLD | The letters written after a name to indicate that person holds a Doctorate in Law. |
| LLM | The letters written after a name to indicate that person holds a Master of Laws. The equivalent course at Oxford University is known as the Bachelor of Civil Law. |
| LPC | The Legal Practice Course, the solicitors' version of the BPTC. |
| Magic Circle | The collective term for what are considered to be the five leading solicitors' firms in the UK (currently Allen & Overy, Clifford Chance, Freshfields, Linklaters, and Slaughter and May). |
| Marshalling | A short period of time spent sitting on the bench with a judge observing cases. |
| Master of the Bench | Distinguished members of an Inn, elected for life, who constitute the Inn's governing body. |
| Mediation | A form of Alternative Dispute Resolution in which an independent third party, known as the mediator, helps the parties involved in a dispute to reach a mutually acceptable resolution. |
| Mess | A group of four sitting in a square dining in an Inn. |

| | |
|---|---|
| Middle Temple | One of the four Inns of Court. |
| Mini-pupillage (a Mini) | A short period of work experience in chambers (see Chapter 11). |
| Moot | A competition in which competitors act as the barristers arguing a legal dispute as if in court. |
| Motion | The subject of argument in a debate. |
| Obiter dictum (plural obiter dicta) | From the Latin meaning "something said in passing", part of a judgment in a case which does not form an essential part of the judge's reasoning and is therefore not binding in future cases. |
| Old Bailey | The Central Criminal Court in London, situated near St. Paul's. |
| OLPAS | The Online Pupillage Application System—the old name for what is now the Pupillage Portal. |
| On the bench | The expression used to indicate where the judge sits in court. |
| On your feet | Another term for doing oral advocacy. |
| Plaintiff | The outdated term for a claimant. |
| Pleadings | The outdated term referring to the documents in which parties set out their positions in advance of an oral hearing, now referred to as Statements of Case. |
| Precedent | A decision of a court which is binding in future cases. |

| | |
|---|---|
| Pro bono | From the Latin meaning "for the common good", this refers to giving free legal advice or representation. |
| Proof or proofs (of evidence) | The outdated term for a witness statement. |
| Pupil | A barrister doing pupillage. |
| Pupillage | This is a one year apprenticeship working as a "pupil" within a chambers. After the first six months, pupils are able to present cases in court. |
| Pupil-Master/Mistress/ Supervisor | A barrister (though not a QC) who supervises a pupil. |
| Pupillage Portal | The central online pupillage application system used by the majority of Chambers. Formerly known as OLPAS. |
| QC | Queen's Counsel, a senior barrister (or sometimes solicitor) who has successfully applied to take silk. Appointments are based on experience and ability. QCs are among the top barristers. Also known as "silks". |
| Qualifying sessions | A selection of events, most commonly dinners, organised by each Inn, which must be completed prior to being called to the Bar. |
| Ratio decendi | Coming from the Latin meaning "the rationale of the decision", ratio refers to the essential part of the reasoning in a judgment which is binding on other courts (the remainder of the case is "obiter dicta"). |

| | |
|---|---|
| Rebut | To argue against a proposition which is put to you, usually by identifying a flaw in that proposition or offering evidence in support of your own. |
| The Royal Courts of Justice or RCJ | The main civil court comprising the High Court and the Civil Division of the Court of Appeal, located on Fleet Street in London. |
| Second six | The second six months of pupillage in which pupils have higher rights of audience and are therefore able to appear in court. |
| The self-employed Bar | The term used to describe barristers in private practice. |
| Senior Junior | An experienced barrister who has not taken silk. |
| Senior or Senior Counsel | A QC or Senior Junior appearing in court with a more junior barrister. |
| Senior status law degree | A two year post-graduate law course giving you the necessary legal qualification to begin the BPTC. |
| Set | Another word for "chambers". |
| Set of chambers | Another expression for "chambers" or "set". |
| Silk | Queen's Counsel, so called because of the silk robes they traditionally wore. |

| | |
|---|---|
| Skeleton Argument | A document briefly outlining your case, and given to the judge and your opposition in advance of the oral hearing. |
| Solicitor-advocate | A solicitor who has taken an additional qualification to gain "higher rights of audience" and is therefore able to appear in the higher courts. |
| Solicitors | The other branch of the legal profession; solicitors advise clients and prepare cases but (unless they are solicitor-advocates), do not have higher rights of audience. |
| Spondee | A student member of a Inn who has been assigned a more senior member of the Inn as a mentor or "sponsor". |
| Sponsor | A barrister allocated to a student member through the Education Department of an Inn to give advice and support. |
| Squatting | A temporary measure whereby, having completed pupillage, you work in a chambers prior to being offered tenancy. |
| Squirrelling | Defining the motion of a debate in an obtusely narrow or obscure way in order to throw the opposition and your own side. |
| Submissions | The arguments presented to a judge. |
| Taken on | Where a pupil is offered a tenancy by chambers. |

| | |
|---|---|
| Taking silk | The act of becoming a QC. |
| Temple | The areas of Middle and Inner Temple located between the Embankment and Fleet Street in London. |
| Tenant | A member of chambers, referred to as a tenant because, as a self-employed practitioner, the payment of rent is obligatory. |
| Third six | A third period of six months' pupillage for pupils who do not get taken on after their second six. It is usually taken in a different set from where the main pupillage took place. |
| Tort | A civil wrong such as negligence. |
| Training Contract | The solicitors' equivalent to pupillage; two years usually spent working for a firm of solicitors. |
| Vacation scheme | The solicitors' equivalent to a mini-pupillage, usually between two weeks and a month working at a solicitors' firm. |
| White wig | A somewhat derogatory term referring to a new barrister (whose wig has not yet been greyed by use). |

# 29 RESOURCES

The following list is to assist you locating further information. The web addresses were correct at the time of going to press.

## Pupillage Listings Guides

The following annual pupillage listings guides are given to students free through the law schools or can be purchased at a legal book shop or on the internet.

(i) *Chambers Student: The Student's Guide to Becoming a Lawyer* (Chambers and Partners)—much of the information within it can also be found at *www.chambersandpartners.com/chambersstudent/index.cfm*.

(ii) *The Training Contract and Pupillage Handbook* (in association with The Trainee Solicitor Group)—available from *www.tcph.co.uk*.

(iii) *The Pupillages Handbook* (gti)—much of the information within it can also be found at *www.pupillages.com*.

(iv) *Target Law* (gti)—updated at www.doctorjob.com/law.

## Legal Directories

(i) *Chambers and Partners* available in hardback or at *www.chambersandpartners.com/uk*.

(ii) *The Legal 500* available in hardback or at *www.legal500.com*.

(iii) *Legal Hub Bar Directory www.legalhub.co.uk/legalhub/app /appinit*.

## Books for Law Students and the Aspiring Barrister

(i) *Bewigged and Bewildered* by Adam Kramer (Hart Publishing).

(ii) *Brief to Counsel* by Henry Cecil—no longer in print but available second hand through libraries or *Amazon.co.uk*, this legal classic is somewhat out of date but nonetheless a joy to read and much of the information about the dynamics between barristers, judges, solicitors, and clerks still holds true.

(iii) *Learning the Law* by Glanville Williams and A.T.H. Smith (Sweet & Maxwell).

(iv) *Letters to a Law Student* by Nicholas McBride (Longman).

(v) *BabyBarista and the Art of War* by Tim Kevan (Bloomsbury).

## Books on Passing the LNAT

(i) *Mastering the National Admissions Test for Law* by Mark Shepherd (Cavendish Publishing).

(ii) *Passing the National Admissions Test for Law* by Rosalie Hutton, Glenn Hutton and Fraser Simpson (Law Matters Publishing).

## Advocacy Texts

(i) *Advocacy in Court: A Beginner's Guide* by Keith Evans (Blackstone Press Ltd).

(ii) *The Devil's Advocate* by Iain Morley (Sweet & Maxwell).

(iii) *The Golden Rules of Advocacy* by Keith Evans (Blackstone Press Ltd).

## Useful Websites

*Training-Related Websites*

(i) *http://ucas.com*—the central organisation for applying to universities in the UK.

(ii) *www.lawcabs.ac.uk*—the central applications website for the GDL.

(iii) *www.lifelonglearning.co.uk/cdl*—Career Development Loans.

*The Inns of Court*

   (i) *www.lincolnsinn.org.uk*

   (ii) *www.innertemple.org.uk*

   (iii) *www.middletemple.org.uk*

   (iv) *www.graysinn.org.uk*

*Practice Area Bar Associations*

   (i) *www.bacfi.org*—Bar Association for Commerce, Finance and Industry.

   (ii) *www.balgps.org.uk*—Bar Association for Local Government and the Public Service.

   (iii) *www.adminlaw.org.uk*—Constitutional and Administrative Law Association.

   (iv) *www.combar.com*—Commercial Bar Association.

   (v) *www.chba.org.uk*—Chancery Bar Association.

   (vi) *www.criminalbar.com*—Criminal Bar Association.

   (vii) *www.piba.org.uk*—Personal Injuries Bar Association.

   (viii) *www.peba.info*—Planning and Environmental Bar Association.

   (ix) *www.pnba.co.uk*—Professional Negligence Bar Association.

   (x) *www.propertybar.org.uk*—Property Bar Association.

   (xi) *www.revenue-bar.org*—Revenue Bar Association.

   (xii) *www.elba.org.uk*—Employment Law Bar Association.

   (xiii) *www.ipba.co.uk*—Intellectual Property Bar Association.

   (xiv) *www.flba.co.uk*—Family Law Bar Association.

   (xv) *www.tecbar.org.uk*—Technology and Construction Bar Association.

*Charities and Other Organisations with Volunteer Opportunities*

    (i) *www.amicus-alj.org*—Amicus, assisting lawyers for justice on Death Row.

    (ii) *www.barprobono.org.uk*—the Bar Pro Bono Unit.

    (iii) *www.citizensadvice.org.uk*—the CAB website.

    (iv) *www.dsc.org.uk*—the Directory of Social Change, information about working in the voluntary sector.

    (v) *www.freerepresentationunit.org.uk*—the Free Representation Unit.

    (vi) *www.icva.org.uk*—Independent Custody Visiting.

    (vii) *www.justice.org.uk*—Justice, the human rights organisation.

    (viii) *www.lawcentres.org.uk*—the Law Centres Federation.

    (ix) *www.liberty-human-rights.org.uk*—Liberty, the human rights organisation.

    (x) *www.noms.homeoffice.gov.uk*—National offender management service.

    (xi) *www.reprieve.org.uk*—Reprieve, fighting for people on Death Row.

    (xii) *www.victimsupport.org.uk*—Victim Support.

*Other Useful Organisations, Societies, Associations and Websites*

    (i) *www.airecentre.org*—Advice on Individual Rights in Europe.

    (ii) *www.aml.org.uk*—Association of Muslim Lawyers.

    (iii) *www.armylegal.co.uk*—the Army Legal Services.

    (iv) *www.att.org.uk*—the Association of Tax Technicians.

    (v) *www.barcouncil.org.uk*—the Bar Council.

    (vi) *www.barstandardsboard.org.uk*—the Bar Standards Board website which features lots of useful information for future barristers.

(vii)   *www.blagg.org*—the Bar Lesbian and Gay Group.

(viii)  *www.cec.org.uk*—the European Commission.

(ix)    *www.cps.gov.uk*—the CPS website.

(x)     *www.dca.gov.uk*—the Department of Constitutional Affairs (now known as the Ministry of Justice) archived webpage.

(xi)    *www.gls.gov.uk*—the Government Legal Service.

(xii)   *www.justice.gov.uk*—the Ministry of Justice.

(xiii)  *www.lag.org.uk*—the Legal Action Group.

(xiv)   *www.lapg.co.uk*—the Legal Aid Practitioners Group.

(xv)    *www.lawcf.org*—the Lawyers' Christian Fellowship.

(xvi)   *www.lcan.org.uk*—Law Careers website.

(xvii)  *www.magistrates-association.org.uk.*

(xviii) *www.pupillages.com*—OLPAS applications.

(xix)   *www.raf.mod.uk/legalservices*—the RAF Legal Services.

(xx)    *www.societyofasianlawyers.com*—the Society of Asian Lawyers.

(xxi)   *www.womenbarristers.co.uk*—the Association for Women Barristers.

*Legal Resources*

(i)   *www.bailii.org*—The British and Irish Legal Information Institute website where you can find British and Irish case law and legislation, European Union case law, Law Commission reports, and other law-related British and Irish material available free. There are also international equivalents which can be found in Bailii's World Resources section.

(ii)  *www.lawcom.gov.uk*—the Law Commission website.

(iii) *www.yale.edu/lawweb/avalon*—Yale University's Avalon Project which contains primary source materials in the numerous fields including Law.

*General Legal Interest*

(i) *http://doctorjob.com/LawGeneral*—the Target Careers website (the people who organise the Target Pupillage Fair and publish the Target Law books series), primarily aimed at solicitors but with plenty of helpful advice.

(ii) *www.barcouncil.org.uk/assets/documents/ItsYourCall.pdf*—a 2005 Bar Council document which still contains applicable advice for those considering a career at the Bar.

(iii) *www.college-of-law.co.uk/assets/pdf/toolkit-for-the-bar.pdf*—the College of Law's student guide for those considering a career at the Bar.

(iv) *www.lawbritannia.co.uk*—a site founded by the former head of careers at one of the largest legal education providers, this site offers an expert careers service and CV assistance as well as a selection of free downloads.

(v) *www.legalweek.com/Home/Default.aspx*—an international website with a section dedicated to the Bar and one for students.

(vi) *www.thelawyer.com/l2b*—the student website attached to The Lawyer (www.the-lawyer.co.uk) newspaper's student offshoot Lawyer2B, filled with legal news, information and advice.

(vii) *www.lawcareers.net*—a comprehensive source of information including a database based on the Training Contract and Pupillage Handbook.

(viii) *www.lawcrossing.co.uk*—a subscription service offering the largest collection of legal jobs in the UK including paralegal positions and holiday work.

(ix) *www.lawgazette.co.uk*—the Law Society's Gazette filled with news and jobs although aimed primarily at solicitors.

(x) *www.prospects.ac.uk/links/ProspectsLaw*—general information about the legal profession including details of pupillages, paralegal positions, holiday work and professional courses.

(xi) *www.rollonfriday.com*—Entertaining site aimed at solicitors.

(xii) *www.spr-consilio.com*—Consilio Magazine, a daily online law magazine for students; the organisation offers excellent revision courses for those taking law exams.

(xiii) *www.timesonline.co.uk/law*—The Times Law Section.

*Mooting and Debating Websites*

(i) *www.britishdebate.com*—Debating website with details of all university debating competitions.

(ii) *www.britishdebate.com/universities/resources/guide-deane. pdf*—A full guide to British debating by Alexander Deane.

(iii) *www.idebate.org/debatabase*—an online database of debating subjects and arguments.

(iv) *www.mootingnet.org.uk*—Mooting resource.

*Blawgs*

There are numerous legal blogs, "blawgs", on the internet at any one time. Many are written by students and offer an excellent insight into the struggles of law school and getting pupillage. Blawgs are constantly changing as writers begin their legal careers or move on to other things so a list of current blawgs would quickly be out of date.

One blawg which is worth a mention however is *http://pupillageand-howtogetit.blogspot.com*. Pupillage and How to Get It is run by Simon Myerson QC of Park Court Chambers and offers a wealth of advice, experience and information for those seeking pupillage.

Bar Standards Board websites referred to in Chapter 27 above

(i) *www.barstandardsboard.org.uk/assets/documents/PTO%20 final%2014–10–08.pdf*

(ii) *http://www.barstandardsboard.rroom.net/about/ourcommittees /qualificationscommittee/applicationforms*

(iii) *www.barstandardsboard.org.uk/Educationandtraining*

# INDEX